Youth Work Ethics

Dedication

The many young people and youth workers who have been part of my life inspire this book.

Titles in the Series

Active Citizenship and Community Learning	ISBN 978 1 84445 152 4
Managing Modern Youth Work	ISBN 978 1 84445 206 4
Law and Youth Work	ISBN 978 1 84445 245 3
Popular Education Practice for Youth and Community Development Work	ISBN 978 1 84445 207 1
Working with Distressed Young People	ISBN 978 1 84445 205 7
Global Youth Work	ISBN 978 1 84445 285 9

To order, please contact our distributor: BEBC Distribution, Albion Close, Parkstone, Poole, BH12 3LL. Telephone: 0845 230 9000, email: learningmatters@bebc.co.uk. You can also find more information on each of these titles and our other learning resources at www.learningmatters.co.uk.

Youth Work Ethics

JONATHAN ROBERTS

Series Editors: Janet Batsleer and Keith Popple

LearningMatters

First published in 2009 by Learning Matters Ltd

British Library Cataloguing in Publication Data
A CIP record for this book is available from the British Library.

ISBN: 978 1 84445 246 0

Cover and text design by Code 5 Design Associates Ltd
Project management by Swales & Willis
Typeset by Swales & Willis, Exeter, Devon
Printed and bound in Great Britain by TJ International Ltd, Padstow, Cornwall

Learning Matters Ltd
33 Southernhay East
Exeter EX1 1 NX
Tel: 01392 215560
info@learningmatters.co.uk
www.learningmatters.co.uk

FSC
Mixed Sources
Product group from well-managed
forests and other controlled sources

Cert no. SGS-COC-2482
www.fsc.org
© 1996 Forest Stewardship Council

Contents

Foreword from the Series Editors

Youth work and community work has a long, rich and diverse history that spans three centuries. The development of youth work extends from the late nineteenth and early twentieth century with the emergence of voluntary groups and the serried ranks of the UK's many uniformed youth organisations, through to modern youth club work, youth project work, and informal education. Youth work remains, in the early twenty-first century, a mixture of voluntary effort and paid and state sponsored activity.

Community work also had its beginnings in voluntary activity. Some of this activity was in the form of 'rescuing the poor', while community action developed as a response to oppressive circumstances and was based on the idea of self-help. In the second half of the twentieth century the state financed a good deal of local authority and government sponsored community and regeneration work and now there are multi-various community action projects and campaigns.

Today there are thousands of people involved in youth work and community work both in paid positions and in voluntary roles. However, the activity is undergoing significant change. National Occupation Standards and a new academic benchmarking statement have recently been introduced, and soon all youth and community workers undertaking qualifying courses and who successfully graduate will do so with an honours degree.

Empowering Youth and Community Work Practice is a series of texts primarily aimed at students on youth and community work courses. However, more experienced practitioners from a wide range of fields will find these books useful because they offer effective ways of integrating theory, knowledge and practice. Written by experienced lecturers, practitioners, and policy commentators each title covers core aspects of what is needed to be an effective practitioner and will address key competences for professional JNC recognition as a youth and community worker. The books use case studies, activities, and references to the latest government initiatives to help readers learn and develop their theoretical understanding and practice. This series then will provide invaluable support to anyone studying or practicing in the field of youth and community work as well as a number of other related fields.

Janet Batsleer
Manchester Metropolitan University

Keith Popple
London South Bank University

Chapter 1

Why worry about ethics in youth work?

C H A P T E R   O B J E C T I V E S

This chapter sets out the broad themes of why ethics is a subject for youth workers to think about. It concludes by outlining the way in which these themes will be explored in more detail in the chapters that follow.

Definitions

Let us start with some definitions from the Oxford English Dictionary.

'Ethics' is the science of morals and comes from a Greek word in part, because of the importance of Aristotle's Ethics in developing the subject.

'Morals' comes from a Latin word used to translate the Greek word 'ethics', and English uses both words alongside each other.

'Morals' in this book will be about the distinction between right and wrong, good and evil. Youth workers need to make moral judgements in the sense that they will need to understand and apply what is right and wrong in a particular setting. Part of developing as a youth work professional involves developing your moral sense and reasoning. You will be faced with complex areas of youth work, and you will need to know what you should and shouldn't do.

All these activities (distinguishing, judging, understanding, applying, sensing, reasoning) are typical of the scientific method. This book will focus on the analysis, reflection, and understanding to help youth workers to be more systematic and thoughtful in their practice. For this reason I will tend to talk about ethics as a rational, scientific approach. 'Moralising' is often used as an objection to unwarranted intervention into others' lives and this can weaken all discussion of right and wrong. I hope that the purpose of this ethical learning will be to create rationales for good youth work.

Good youth work

Ethics is about 'good youth work'. It helps sort out what we ought to do. We are so used to a management of youth work that talks about 'excellent practice' and 'appropriate behaviour' that we could assume the whole area is already sorted out and only needs addressing to keep philosophically minded academics on courses happy and occupied. Ethics informs management by providing 'practice principles' to be carried out by professional workers. But this is not the end of ethics. Ethics informs the interior life of the worker beyond the reach of management. A youth worker needs to know for his or her own satisfaction if he or she has done good youth work. This interior life may be important as workers move from one short contract to the next and seek a connecting purposeful narrative for their working life. Ethics encourages good work with young people at a finer level of discernment than management decisions. People other than managers want to know if what we choose to do is good.

Facts and values

Ethicists distinguish between 'fact' and 'value' (Ramsay, 1967, p111). This ethical distinction is important in youth work. What 'is' the case and what 'ought' to be are practical differences that face youth services all the time. The 'ought' judgements separate good and right, from bad and wrong. Facts may be difficult, but they can be seen in a different category to the values. The facts are that young people are growing up in communities, influenced by their families, schools, commercial markets, and prospects of work. Social scientists help us understand the detail and analyse the interaction of these facts. Youth work intervenes into these facts to express values. The values want to see the development of young people, not just the reproduction of their existing social state. The values want to see greater equality and inclusion, not just the same power relations. The values describe youth work learning as informal and distinguish it from the instrumental processes of much of the learning young people experience. These and other values encourage youth workers to persist in trying to achieve what is right. In the grammar of youth work the facts are the 'nouns' and the values are the 'verbs'. The facts or nouns are the things we must name and deal with. The values or the 'verbs' are the doing words, the activities, the movement and the energies of our work.

CASE STUDY

The Mill Youth Centre

The youth centre has been in that part of town for years. The apprentices from the works used to come in and play snooker and five-a-side when they finished their shift. Later it was a good place for the unemployed young men to meet for cups of tea and basketball during the long days of doing nothing. Now it is used by a project during the day to work with young people, mostly boys, who are excluded from school.

A new worker is appointed and is told that it is a cushy number provided they get the pool balls out and keep the coffee bar books balanced. In their diary they write:

Like: building and location, exclusion project.

Dislike: mainly male, too much recreation, not much sign of learning, no sign of being part of the bigger world. Feels like a waiting room for the old people's home.

ACTIVITY **1.1**

- *What are the facts faced by this worker?*
- *What are the values they wish to express?*

Rigid codes or responsive practice

Ethicists investigate the extent to which ethical statements are objective (Ramsey, 1967, p 111f). This is important for youth workers. On the one hand management structures, National Occupational Standards (NOS), ethical codes, and professional status all appear to make youth work as objective as possible. Youth support workers undertaking a National Vocational Qualification (NVQ) collect a series of observations of their youth work practice. This builds up in a rigid structure so that we know that the worker is competent, and has embedded the values of youth work in practice. On the other hand youth workers know that they are flexible as professionals. They adapt to different settings, respond as far as possible to individual young people, and express their own identity as a particular sort of youth worker. More complicatedly, sometimes an emotional response might be very important. As a result, the range and variety of youth workers' practice can seem and feel very subjective. This contrast between rigid, defined competency and flexible, emotional intelligence can bring trouble. Managers inside the organisation dress up their frustration by accusing well-intentioned youth workers of 'inappropriate behaviour'. Observers outside youth work look at us and say that we don't know what we are about. We need to explore the relationships between the rigid objective statements that all youth workers share and the flexible, responsive practice that looks subjective. Values are part of shared youth work practice and youth work needs to be built on strong moral foundations.

Being professional

Professionals work with skill and discernment basing their practice on values that have been developed with other people. Professionals make their choices about right and wrong, good and bad, on the basis of what they know about other professionals who work in similar settings of complexity and ambiguity. Making the step from collecting competencies to professional behaviour allows us to respond to the consequences of complexity and ambiguity.

Consider what we need to take into account when we work with others. Firstly, the method we use to work with others. It is not always obvious how things will turn out and so a simple mechanism will not be sufficient. We will need to have a range of approaches available to us, and to have the capacity to think through and respond to the changing circumstances. Secondly, the focus on benefiting the young person we are working with. Professionals deal with others to try to give them the best possible result. The interests of that person and the interests of the organisation employing the youth worker may not always coincide. Thirdly, the focus on how long it might take. Time scales for the effect of a piece of work will vary. It may be best to interview pensioners (Jeffs, 2003, p135) to get a real grasp of the long term impact of youth work on a person's life. A simple management proposal of how to achieve a particular end result will not allow for these changes in method, responses to the needs of the young person, or even the unknown nature of long term influences. Ethics is a good way of talking through what we try to do as youth workers.

Key idea: Aristotle – reflecting on professional behaviour

To highlight the benefits of good relationships Aristotle distinguishes between the following:

- friendship based on utility: I am friends with them because I get something in return;
- friendship based on pleasure: I am friends with them because they give me pleasure;
- friendship based on goodness: I am friends with them because of who they are.

For youth workers utility means: they do the job to get paid. They go through the motions and meet the requirements of the rather limited rule book.

For young people utility can be seen in using the youth work only to gain accredited awards and entries for their CV to overcome their weakness in mainstream education. This is hard for youth workers who are usually proud of their contribution to young people's social capital.

For youth workers pleasure can mean disaster: not long ago there were men in the service who delighted in the pleasure given them by teenage girls; stronger rules about sexual abuse made this illegal and unacceptable. Youth workers may programme activities that are their personal favourites (under the guise of competence) but may not provide the best learning for young people.

For young people pleasure might mean responding to jolly trips out. They go to Amsterdam but won't talk to Dutch young people.

For youth workers goodness means sticking with young people for themselves and showing personal integrity.

For young people goodness is the growing appreciation of the long-term commitment of the youth service to work for their benefit without imposing other people's agendas.

What examples can you think of?

Aristotle's distinctions help us separate the short term from the long term. When we plan we seek short-term outputs and long-term outcomes (*Nicomachean Ethics Book VIII Chapter 3*).

What influences the ethics of youth work?

Historical youth work practice

The first influence is the practice of youth work. Youth work began as a reflective profession, arguably, in 1844 with the founding of the Young Men's Christian Association (YMCA) by George Williams. Since then there have been reports, analyses of practice, training programmes, and the development of qualifications. All of these express in different ways the values and ethical choices youth work makes. This history provides stable reference points for workers to assess what is essential about youth work and what is simply a proposal from another discipline.

Ethical codes

The second influence is the collection of ethical codes that apply to youth work. Anyone undertaking a qualification that uses the National Occupational Standards in youth work is faced with the twelve youth work values agreed with the Sector Skills Council 'Life Long Learning UK'. These values are improvements of statements made over several decades, and it is possible to place classic statements of youth work, like Scouting for Boys (Baden-Powell, 1908), alongside them. Next, the National Youth Agency (NYA) has a set of eight ethical principles (NYA, 1999). We will return to them later in the book. Finally, there is the United Nations (UN) Convention on the Rights of the Child (UN, 1989). These 54 articles define the rights of those under 18 and the ways in which those rights are to be secured. This international statement has been developed since the First World War and has reformed the legal frameworks that apply to youth work. We will discuss its application throughout the book. Youth workers are among the professionals competent to advocate the rights described.

Historical summary of the development of the UN Convention on the Rights of the Child

- April 1915: Suffragette associations in the warring and neutral countries organized a peace conference in The Hague bringing together about 1 200 women.

- 19 May 1919: in the Royal Albert Hall, London, Save the Children was founded and received among its first donations £10 000 from British miners to help the starving children in Vienna.

- 1923: Eglantine Jebb at Save the Children publishes five children's rights.

  1 The child must be given the means requisite for its normal development, both materially and spiritually.

  2 The child that is hungry must be fed, the child that is sick must be helped, the child that is backward must be helped, the delinquent child must be reclaimed, and the orphan and the waif must be sheltered and succoured.

  3 The child must be the first to receive relief in times of distress.

  4 The child must be put in a position to earn a livelihood, and must be protected against every form of exploitation.

5 The child must be brought up in the consciousness that its talents must be devoted to the service of its fellow men.

- 1924: the League of Nations supports these by the Declaration of Geneva.

- 1948: the United Nations Declaration of Human Rights is agreed.

- 20 November 1959: the United Nations agrees a statement of ten rights of the child.

- 1978: Poland leads a proposal at the UN to develop a treaty about children's rights.

- 20 November 1989: the adoption of the UN Convention on the Rights of the Child.

- 26 January 1990: the first 61 countries sign the treaty.

Discernment with other people

The third influence is the social networks, partners and stakeholders where we operate and which set the character of the work we do. These are important because they may separate youth workers united by the first two sets of influences. For example: Save the Children, or the Society of the Sacred Heart operate across national boundaries and will draw on a global perspective in making local decisions. In contrast, local authority or neighbourhood practice will be specifically concerned with a local agenda.

Other institutions and organisations in society may not be youth work based but may bring a new focus on values and priorities for youth workers. For example: accidents, bad practice, or disputes about the relationship between professionals and growing adolescents may lead to investigations, reports, court judgements and recommendations. Ethical debates that might be open to several interpretations are subject to public dissection. Clear guidance about a publicly acceptable approach then gives confidence to those who argue one way and deter those who argue differently. We will look at, for example, House of Lords judgements that have moved youth work practice on in important areas of ethics. Finally, social organisations express in long-term ways some of the philosophical themes that we will look at next. Democracy is not just an idea in a book, it has institutions with procedures designed to make it work as a lived reality. We have skilfully made ways of expressing values and principles in our social organisations (Dunstan, 1974).

Philosophy

The fourth influence is the philosophical reflection on ethics. Many ethics books would put this higher up the league table. It is useful to use philosophy's habits of careful thought and traditions to define certain principles and approaches. Here are four examples.

1 Aristotle wants us to live a good life and this virtue requires wise decisions, which his 'Ethics' can help think through.

2 Kant encourages us to look for a 'categorical imperative', a principle that I carry out because it ought to be a universal law (Kant, 1997, p31): respecting persons, never lying or manipulating, and so on.

3 Utilitarians like Bentham and Mill ask us about the wider consequences of what we do for others; how to calculate the greatest good for the greatest number?

4   John Rawls advocates the use of rights which everybody has equally. It is part of being human that we have fair treatment from others, and that our right to particular behaviours is not restricted because of who we are. (Rawls, 1971)

CASE STUDY

UN Convention on the Rights of the Child (youth-friendly text)

Article 22: If you are a child who has come into a country as a refugee, you should have the same rights as children born in that country.

Article 30: You have a right to learn and use the language and customs of your family whether or not these are shared by the majority of the people in the country where you live.

Article 39: If you have been neglected or abused, you should receive special help to restore your self-respect.

These three examples of UN Articles can be considered in the light of Kantian categorical imperatives. A child has these rights and we will uphold them. Therefore all children we encounter have these rights. In developing this moral reasoning we have developed our own responses to children in our society (we will not employ them in factories). We have also responded to boundary crossing incidents: we looked after the 85,000 Jews who escaped Hitler by coming to the UK.

Try them instead as Utilitarian ethics. They look like proposals that go against the interests of the greatest number. Welcoming 'dispersed' asylum seekers from Iraq or Uganda in areas of great local need, unused to diverse populations can be disruptive for the majority. These new people seem inconvenient, using up services in uneconomic ways: why do we have to change our systems, notices and provision for them? These are the questions of the majority seeking their own good.

Rights are not easy for majorities. But they are the residues of human experiences. We know that the countries (for example, Denmark) that tried to save their entire Jewish population from the European majority rule did a good thing.

Synthesising different elements

Youth workers may decide to adopt one of these approaches. You may look at the historical settings of the philosophers and consider the extent to which our society already expresses so many of their abstract hopes. For example, the National Health Service does express the categorical imperative of caring for the sick, and seeks to achieve the greatest good for the greatest number: our current problems lie in the detail. Philosophy can sometimes present blueprints to reform a past society aspects of which we have long sorted out and are now faced with new dilemmas.

Some youth workers come with blueprints of their own. You might be sufficiently inspired by the values expressed by a youth worker or organisation that you want to be rooted in the specific developed practice of that youth work. Other youth workers encounter the philosophers and think they are a weak version of a faith they already hold. Their own belief will determine the priorities they set for behaviour. The challenge for youth work ethics is to enable all youth workers to express the reasons for their choices.

Who are ethics important for in youth work?

Learning about ethics is important for youth workers so that they can explain their decisions to other people. Think about the stakeholders who genuinely ask you questions about your youth work. Who might be interested in listening to the reasons you give for the choices you've made?

You

The first person that needs to understand why you do something is you. If you don't have good reasons and a sense of the balance required in complex work then you will make mistakes, give up, or not serve young people well. If you can't explain it to yourself, what chance do you have explaining it to anyone else? In your private reflections you might write contradictory ideas out at length, you may consider questions that you will find hard to answer, you may need to go away and read some background material. You may then 'boil down' some of these thoughts into key elements that will be useful clear explanations for people not trained as a youth worker. Brevity for others comes from careful preparation and thorough reflection.

Young people

Second, you ought to be able to explain it to the young person who you are working with. They may not want all the detail, but some of it may need to come out in terms of the boundaries of what can be done. Whoever looks after the young person will also need to understand what you are doing.

Youth work managers

Next, the people involved in the formal management of the work do need to know and understand what you are doing. This will often involve partner agencies as well as your management committee or line managers. We will think about accountability later in the book.

The public

Finally, the wider public want to know that what you are doing is a good thing. Your ethical reasons are ones which others can share and support in a variety of ways. If you explain how the methods and purposes of your work are good and important for the young people and the wider society you give others the chance to join what you are doing as they too judge it to be the right thing to do. Some may write legislation, others organise money, some may redecorate the place you meet in or be willing to speak up for you when the rota is being redrawn for lettings: whatever the response you will know that your ethical leadership has been taken up by others and had a good effect.

How can we think about ethics in youth work?

Good ethical decision making and explanation in youth work needs to be sufficiently practical and allow for the complexity we have already identified. Youth work is a reflective, informal, educational discipline and can draw on educational themes. The interaction between reflection and action makes a cyclical approach a powerful way of developing youth work: starting with a dilemma from the work, reflecting on it and drawing ways forward from the analysis, applying the conclusions to the work, and later starting the process of reflection again. Youth work is also a caring intervention in communities and can draw on the experience of allied disciplines such as social work, counselling, and church pastoral work. Ready-made theoretical structures will help you test your own processes. There are variations on Kolb's cycle of experience, reflection and learning (Banks and Nohr, 2003, p64), or a seven stage plan (Goovaerts in Banks and Nohr, p88ff). Such structures of reflection can take thinking beyond the level of just identifying principles (typical of first year undergraduate study), through critical exploration (second year), to making sound independent judgements (third year), perhaps at the leading edge of youth work practice (postgraduate).

Kane proposes a cycle of reflection (1986, p86) with eight elements allowing different critical elements to be taken in a particular sequence that allows for the variation in objectivity of the judgement criteria. She asks questions about the perception of the facts, followed by insights from disciplines of critical understanding which might be widely shared (such as social sciences), and concludes with insights from the most specific form of insight, the faith perspective. This approach avoids privileging closed sets of values over discussion that is likely to be more open to a wider range of people. It is a practical response to the epistemological difference between the 'is' of facts and the 'ought' of a particular ethical approach.

This cycle develops arguments for good youth work. It distinguishes between fact and value. It considers the wider influences on the situation and then focuses on youth work's distinctive contribution. It begins from a dilemma in practice and returns to inform that dilemma.

ACTIVITY 1.2

Work in a group of three or four to address a dilemma that is difficult to resolve in the strategic development of your youth work. Use the cycle on page 10 and try to keep moving round the cycle by doing one stage at a time and spending between five and ten minutes on each phase.

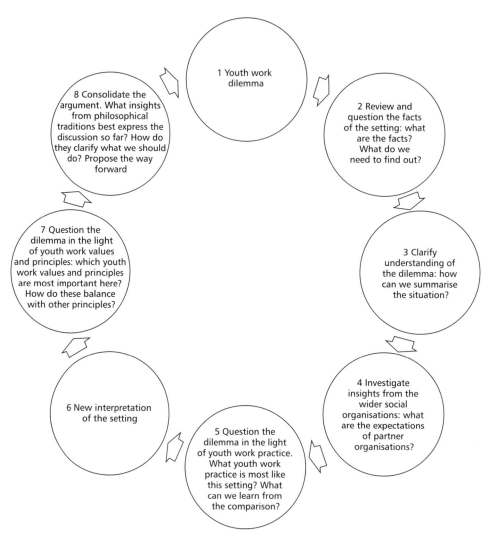

Figure 1.1 A cycle that draws together elements from these reflective approaches and the influences identified earlier

Where do we need to discuss ethics of youth work?

Youth work learning

Youth work courses are places where youth workers get the chance to talk through ethics. Good learning programmes ought to have space for this to happen. The problem is that college is also the last place many youth workers talk through ethics. Once the essay has been written or the ethics learning outcome achieved in the reflection on youth work practice it can be abandoned with the other arcane material which appears in the curriculum to provide hurdles to professional qualification. My hope is that youth work courses provide a still point in a busy turning world where youth workers get an experience of reflection and supported discussion that they will continue to seek as part of their professional practice. I know that other course leaders share this hope of rigorous moral education and that we see our work as part of the wider youth work field. Jefts and Spence, for example, note that:

> It has been impossible for CETYCW and the ETS to address the remaining concern of the Thompson Report that existing courses were focusing unduly on the need to carry students through programmes rather than prioritising their preparation for the morally and intellectually challenging work they would encounter after graduation.
>
> (Jeffs and Spence, 2008, p155)

So, where can ethical discussion find a place outside the academic setting?

Supervision

In the field a common place to dissect ethical dilemmas is in supervision sessions. Many workers find formal management sessions focus on achieving what is needed or agreed. Youth workers should still maintain that excellent practice of meeting with someone outside their work for 'non-managerial supervision'. Finding another youth worker who will meet up once every six weeks for an hour to talk through a subject with some rigour is a powerful way of developing professional practice and staying with challenging work when isolated and hard pressed. If you have not had the opportunity to be well supervised, making an agreement with a fellow student can be helpful. There is good literature available (for example Hawkins and Shohet, 2000), and there are courses to help train supervisors.

Management meetings

A good management committee can provide a place to talk ethics through with others. A cycle like the one shown in Figure 1.1 requires enough time and a willingness to ask open questions to get to the heart of the different stages, while moving the discussion on to address the whole cycle. It is not a philosophy club, but a discussion that decides why and how the next piece of youth work will be undertaken. The best discussions include ideas of what to monitor to review the effectiveness of the work in achieving the moral ambition of the group.

Reports to the wider public

Good youth projects tell their supporters about what they have been doing and how good youth work tries to do good things. People want to be part of making the world a better place for young people. A report that explains the ups and downs of trying to achieve this will include everyone in the consequences of this hope. Learning how to do good things better is a good moral activity. Consider the way in which charities that used to 'collect sixpences for black babies' now express their work in terms of reciprocity and sharing resources across the globe to achieve justice for all.

C H A P T E R   R E V I E W

In this introduction I have described youth work as a moral activity. Ethics is about choosing good actions. It is influenced by youth work history, formal codes, groups we are part of and philosophy. We blend the ingredients to make good youth work. The best blend comes from conversation with young people, managers and wider society. Ethics are more reliable when their contradictions are carefully thought through. This book will help you do this.

Here is a brief summary of the way this book looks at the areas of ethical debate.

- Chapters 2, 3 and 4 look at the major values of youth work: association, listening, equality and taking part in society.

- Chapter 5 addresses the ways in which the groups of young people we work with are the settings for learning about right and wrong by young people.

- Chapter 6 focuses on the NYA code of practice for youth workers.

- Chapter 7 reflects on the way projects are developed and managed by stakeholders, and the way that purpose can be maintained and developed.

- Chapter 8 looks at the central issue of finding evidence and using it.

- Chapter 9 draws together the elements of the discussion and looks at effective ways of balancing contradictory demands.

FURTHER READING

Aristotle (2000) *Nicomachean ethics.* This is the first, and persistently influential, ethics book. Aristotle's first hearers 'were people who could have made a difference', and Aristotle is insistent that his lectures are practical in intent. (Introduction, viii) Youth workers can start reading Aristotle in Books VIII and IX, which discuss friendship.

MacIntyre, A (1966) *A short history of ethics; from the Homeric era to the twentieth century.* London: Routledge and Kegan Paul. A lucid account.

Robinson, D and Garratt, C (1999) *Introducing ethics.* Duxford: Icon Books. Presented in a graphic book format it is, perhaps, the most compact digest of a wide range of philosophical approaches to ethics including some good examples. If you have never studied ethics this is not a bad place to start.

Thompson, M (1999) *Ethical theory.* London: Hodder and Stoughton. A brief survey of the main ethical theories.

REFERENCES

Aristotle (2000) *Nicomachean ethics*, Crisp R (ed) Cambridge: Cambridge University Press.

Banks, S and Nohr, K (2003) *Teaching practical ethics for the social professions.* Odder: FESET.

Boehmer, E (2004) Baden-Powell, R (1908) *Scouting for boys.* Oxford: Oxford University Press.

Dunstan, GR (1974) *The artifice of ethics.* London: SCM Press.

Goovaerts, H (2003) Working with a staged plan, in Banks, S and Nohr, K (eds), *Teaching practical ethics for the social professions*. Odder: FESET.

Hawkins, P and Shohet, R (2000) *Supervision in the helping professions*. Maidenhead: Open University Press.

Jeffs, T (2003) Basil Henriques and the 'house of friendship', in Gilchrist, R, Jeffs, T and Spence, J (eds) *Architects of change*. Leicester: Youth Work Press.

Jeffs, T and Spence, J (2008) Farewell to all that. *Youth and Policy* 97 and 98.

Kane, M (1986) *What kind of God?* London: SCM Press.

Kant, I (1997) *Groundwork of the metaphysics of morals*. Cambridge: Cambridge University Press.

Ramsay, IT (1967) Ethical language, in Macquarie, JA (ed) *Dictionary of Christian Ethics*. London: SCM Press.

Rawls, J (1971) *A theory of justice*. Cambridge, MA: Belknap Press of Harvard University.

Chapter 2

Values: association and listening

C H A P T E R   O B J E C T I V E S

In this chapter I will explore two youth work values that express society's desire to have good things happen for young people.

1 Association: a commitment to devise settings for young people to meet and develop.

2 Listening: a commitment to make opportunities for young people to say what is on their mind.

Both activities are what we expect to be able to do as free individuals in a democratic society. They are normal adult interactions in the public sphere and our society values protects, and encourages them. In fact, because of the way in which public time, money, and effort are spent on them we can know that they are seen to be good. In this chapter the ethical test we can use is: if it is good for all citizens of this society, then it is good for young people to do. By the end of this chapter you should be able to:

* identify what each theme means;

* explain how each theme links to the ethical codes;

* analyse the wider benefits for society of these youth work themes.

Links to the National and Professional Occupational Standards for Youth Work 2008

Values	Principle activity area	Examples of Units
Association and listening	1. Facilitate personal, social and educational development of youngpeople	1.1.2, 1.1.3, 1.1.4, 1.1.5, 1.1.6, 1.1.7, 1.2.1, 1.2.2, 1.2.3, 1.2.4, 1.3.1, 1.3.2, 1.3.3, 3.1.1, 3.1.2, 4.2.3, 4.2.6

Youth work is a good activity carried out in society to express right actions by society. In Chapters 2, 3 and 4 we will explore four values typical of youth work: association, listening to young people, equality of opportunity, and participation. These values need to be set in the context of why we should do anything good for young people in the first place. We will start by contrasting society's views about doing good youth work with its views about bad young people. Youth work exists in morally contested places.

Youth work in society's moral debates

Friday night

It is a bleak Friday evening as I leave the house. I am looking forward to the evening with the young people. Good youth work will be putting a smile on the faces of the young people and their parents as they get ready. There will be new people there tonight who have heard that it is a good way to spend Friday nights. A ward councillor will be dropping by – youth work is an important part of the Children's Services. I turn the corner and see the lights shining on the newly polished floor: this is a good job, I'm glad I do it.

Youth work is an ethical choice

Youth work is an ethical activity. It makes choices to do good things. Youth workers talk about 'good youth work' and generally they mean well-planned and managed youth work; they are already inside the assumption that 'we will do youth work'. This chapter steps outside youth work to look at the alignment of ethical choices that are made when youth work happens. Youth work is a value judgement made in society, not a fact. Each generation and each neighbourhood has to say: *we ought to have some youth work.*

Youth work's stakeholders sharing a choice to do good

Let us name the people in the case study who are engaged with this ethical choice.

The young people decide that this is the way they want to spend Friday evening. It will be a good time. They have been looking forward to it. It is a chosen and planned part of their life.

Their parents are pleased about the youth project. Their child (who they worry about) is making a good choice: they learn more about life in good ways, they meet new friends, their horizons are widened, and so on. Their child is also not making a bad choice: they are not getting drunk, falling into fights, at risk of dying, and so on.

The councillor likes youth work because it does good things for the neighbourhood. The youth centre allows him to meet young people so that he can hear their views about the area, and this helps democratic governance. He likes the good things the young people do with each other and for the neighbourhood. Last week they had a group from their twin town: they lived the reality of international friendship. A modest amount of public money avoids petty crime that springs up when the kids are bored, and leaves the police free to deal with bigger problems. It also addresses the Local Authority duty under the 2006 Education and Inspections Act to secure: *(b) sufficient recreational leisure-time activities which are for the improvement of their [13–19 year olds] well-being, and sufficient facilities for such activities.*

The cleaner is proud to work there. She is pleased to do something good for the bairns and remembers with affection meeting her husband under the mirror ball a few years back. She is happy to listen to what they say and to help out.

Finally, there is the youth worker; who is pleased to work these odd hours because it means that the young people get the best out of their lives. This book will continue to explore the many reasons youth workers might have for doing the good that is youth work.

The fact of a building or a budget may not make youth work happen. Even a legal duty placed on a Local Authority does not create a duty for all the other stakeholders in youth work. Each stakeholder will make a choice.

Youth work in opposition to bad perceptions of young people

You do not have to look far to find bad stories about young people. Stan Cohen (1974/2002) captured society's fascination in his book about Mods and Rockers, *Folk Devils and Moral Panics*. Young people in public places are seen as trouble. A cycle of conversation about them in the adult population raises frightening fantasies of the evil they might do. This creates an appetite for stories of young people who behave illegally and violently. Mayhew made his name 150 years ago with similar investigations: *I have met with boys and girls to whom a gaol had no terrors (Mayhew, 1985, p182)*.

Youth work is in dialogue with this miserable vision of young people. Youth work claims to be a cure for this badness. Youth work is attacked as being too slow to judge good and bad. The conversation is often so heated and ill thought out that youth workers retreat and hope to get on with their young people out of public scrutiny. But there is common ground. In conversation we can begin to make a common place and develop different themes in the dialogue.

Association

Definition and meaning

Association seems a dull word, only used as an initial (FA, YMCA), or a counselling cue. The dictionary first finds it in 1535 to describe a confederation or league of people; by the next century it is used both for formal organisations to achieve a common purpose (advance science), and in the more general sense of friendship. That crossover between organisations to do good things and friendship suits youth work well. George Williams organised the first YMCA in 1844 so that young men could meet and develop, association was to be purposeful and life enhancing, not accidental. We share that purposeful approach to youth work. The key purpose of youth work is to:

> *Enable young people to develop holistically, working with them to facilitate their personal, social and educational development, to enable them to develop their voice, influence and place in society and to reach their full potential.*
>
> (National Occupational Standards, 2008)

Youth work is intentional. It is chosen as an activity and a method. As such, it is not just a group of young people in a place of their choosing. Association expresses purpose both on the part of the young people and the adults who support them.

John Rawls: morality and association

Rawls described association as a key process in moral development (1971, p467ff). Each person learns moral standards appropriate the role in each association to which they belong. Typical associations include family, school, neighbourhood, and the shorter term co-operation of games and play.

Young people develop intellectual skills by association (here Rawls follows Flavell). They recognise people have different points of view. People have different wants and ends, plans, and motives. They have to find out these from what people say and how they act. Overall, they are assessing other people. They also have to control their own behaviour in response to the wider group. Developing and using those skills of sympathy, empathy and restraint are important tasks in youth work.

Importantly for us, young people also develop moral skills by associating with others. Certainly, they see people behaving badly: manipulating or exploiting others; and the question is 'how does the association manage this?' They also experience the friendship of being in an organisation that we call belonging. Belonging means that they trust and rely on one another; they live up to what the others expect them to do. Rules may be set that define fairness and when rules are broken there is the response of the individual not only in terms of personal guilt, but also in terms of reparation to the group (Rawls, 1971, p470).

Rawls concludes that there is an important structure of justice at the heart of society's associations and institutions. By associating we learn the morality of association. We view each other as equals (see Chapter 3): *joined together in a system of cooperation known to be for the advantage of all and governed by a common conception of justice* (Rawls, 1971, p472). There are cooperative virtues: *justice and fairness, fidelity and trust, integrity and impartiality. Typical vices are graspingness and unfairness, dishonesty and deceit, prejudice and bias* (Rawls, 1971, p472).

Niebuhr (1932) argues for a moral distinction between the moral behaviour of individuals and the moral behaviour of groups. Aristotle's arguments about friendship (Chapter 1) help us with the moral behaviour of individuals. Rawls' arguments about association help us understand the moral behaviour of groups.

The right of association in the UN Convention, and its practice in youth work history
The UN Convention Article 15:

> States Parties recognize the rights of the child to freedom of association and to freedom of peaceful assembly.

> No restrictions may be placed on the exercise of these rights other than those imposed in conformity with the law and which are necessary in a democratic society in the

interests of national security or public safety, public order, the protection of public health or morals or the protection of the rights and freedoms of others.

This article extends to children the rights of assembly and freedom of assembly enjoyed by adults. It reflects in part the real legal person that is the child under 18, they are not extensions of their parents, but are people in their own right. In a dramatic global setting, the Article affirms the protest of the pupils of Soweto in 1976 against the apartheid regime, and the part these young people played in a long struggle for equality and democracy. In a modest way, it reflects the historical reality of youth organisations in the UK going about their activities in a peaceful way: a jazz band led by a troupe of majorettes or a Boys Brigade parade would both be watched with smiles and admiration as they go down the street.

The Albemarle report constructed a youth service in England and Wales for the 14–20 year olds of the baby boom; a generation without National Service to keep them off the streets (1960, p13). The first activity the report names for young people is 'association' (1960, p52ff). Here are five aspects that they highlighted.

1 *To encourage young people to come together in groups of their own choosing is the fundamental task of the service (paragraph 184).*

2 *Association requires young people to commit themselves to membership (paragraph 185).*

3 *Association provides a setting where young people can get the 'counsel' (paragraph 187) that they might lack now that they are in work (A link to the second value in this chapter).*

4 *Association leads to self determination: 'we value very highly the active participation of the young and their own leadership of groups they bring into existence themselves' (paragraph 188). A link to Chapter 4.*

5 *Association needs suitable facilities. More than the old fashioned gymnasium, table tennis room, canteen or hall: 'an approximation to the facilities for social life offered by a college union' (paragraph 190).*

The Albemarle report was presented to Parliament in February 1960 and set the tone for much youth work that followed. Civil servants preparing the Education and Inspections Act 2006 went back to the text and considered its central themes.

CASE STUDY

The new estate

The farm sat on the south bank of a large river separated from the old settlement by a tributary. The developers saw it as prime building land for family housing. Families were attracted by the fact that it was out of the way of the rest of the conurbation: free from joy riders, theft, and the noise of a community where unemployment meant other families didn't keep working hours. The local councillors had other things on their minds: more troubled areas.

CASE STUDY *continued*

Now the estate has a single road on and off and lots of families happy in their new homes. The small children have a delightful new primary school which is thriving. There are a few shops, but little else. Residents are campaigning to improve transport links.

The teenagers' schools are elsewhere, but back on the estate they want to meet. The police are baffled when asked to confront these polite and pleasant groups of young people who are meeting to talk. Parents are embarrassed to find their child report an encounter with the law; they aren't rich, but they are decent hard working people.

The council reviews who is living on the estate and finds it has one of the highest rates of teenagers anywhere in the Borough. There is no 'historic project'. There is no high risk targeted group. They decide to form a partnership with voluntary groups and residents to build somewhere for young people to meet.

ACTIVITY 2.1

- *What is the single good thing that needs to be achieved for young people in this case?*
- *Who are the stakeholders?*
- *Why will each stakeholder consider it a good thing to support the new project.*

Association and interventions by youth workers: comparisons

Association seems a weak word to describe an intervention by professionals. Consider six forms of intervention into young people's lives:

1. the 15,000 hours (Rutter, 1979) of compulsory treatment by mainstream education;
2. the power of arrest of a police officer;
3. the imposition of an Anti-Social Behaviour Order;
4. the removal of a young person from their family by a social worker;
5. participation in a training programme run by the Fire and Rescue service for young arsonists;
6. access to training programmes and money managed by advisors.

ACTIVITY 2.2

On our youth work course we form lines of students representing different people who work with young people and then we ask them to agree a scale of increasing powers to rank the different roles. Try this using the six forms of invention, adding other roles you know, and see where youth workers are placed in the ranking.

Living with weakness

Youth work practice is generally based on managing weakness of intervention into other people's lives. Good youth workers choose this: 'I don't want to be a. . .', 'I don't want the sort of control exercised by a. . .' They choose this weaker more vulnerable approach to young people. Power is important to achieve some good things in society: fire fighters need to be decisive and effective in a fire; a social worker needs to be able to challenge family behaviour to protect the vulnerable. But youth workers try to make a place where young people can begin to try out their adult power. Youth workers are adult professionals who choose weakness so that young people can find their feet as adults. It is a good thing that youth work helps young people become effective adults, youth workers may need to back off to allow this to happen.

Don't be seduced by power games

Managing your own power is not straightforward. Poor workers get tempted to adopt some strength tactic. Maybe they do it to overcome their dissatisfaction with their work, or maybe because there is a power culture at work and they have to perform for rivals in the Civic Centre (Handy, 1985, p188ff). They talk in these units of power: *Our project has a huge budget* or *No one tries it on with me.* I think that they have become more interested in their relations with their adult peers than the young people they are meant to work with. It is a bad sign when the youth worker is always in the office, or addresses young people over the top of their briefcase or Blackberry. Their mind is on a power structure other than the power relation between them and the young person in front of them. Thinking about ethics helps youth workers stick with the task: a good power relation is a slightly vulnerable one, a good approach (and there is more on this later) is to listen.

Facilitating young people's choices

The first of 12 values that distinguish youth work from other, sometimes related activities involving young people is:

> Young people choose to be involved, not least because they want to relax, meet friends, make new relationships, to have fun, and to find support.
>
> (National Occupational Standards, 2008, value 1)

The choice that young people make is the starting point for all youth work. It is a choice they make every time they take part. This value is the top of the list for youth workers and reminds us that it is more important than anything else. Choosing is what adults do. We want the young people we work with to become excellent adults and one of the choices they will make, we hope, is to manage without youth work. When young people don't make this choice we might say that they are too dependent on us or our organization. Bruce Reed (1978) encouraged workers faced with dependency to practice an oscillation between dependency and autonomy to encourage free choices to be made.

But when we start with a young person they are not adults yet and we are. Coming into any new group can be hard. They may not be able, on their own, to *relax, meet friends, make new relationships, to have fun, and to find support*. Difficult, dominant people might make them anxious, prove difficult to get to know, frighten or bore them; and they may feel pretty isolated. The youth worker is there to encourage good relations to flourish between individuals. I still collect name games for groups to play together so that finding out who is who is done easily. I like exercises where groups get to know each other at a deeper and deeper level because the friendships, relationships, and support won't be something they choose without that depth. The French word *facile* means *easy*. Youth workers facilitate, make easier, the choices that young people make.

Young people's choice can seem like a reinforcement of the weakness of youth work. How will we be sure that they turn up? The answer to that is to be found in the other values: young people will be interested in what is done, and how, and the relationships they have built up with each other and the youth worker that they choose to do, and choose to be reliable. Good youth work leads to young people behaving in a grown up, adult responsible way.

Choice is a real strength in youth work compared with some of the other processes applied to young people. MacDonald and Marsh report the downsides as well the benefits of compulsion for young people: a girl in a low achieving class in a low achieving school being taken to weight training by the maths teacher (2005, p50), or badly behaved boys being sent to a learning support base where they coloured in dinosaurs with wax crayons (2005, p51), or *I feel forced a bit, because I didn't have no choice really. . . if I didn't do it [New Deal], they'd stop your benefit'* (2005, p98). The more that young people's opportunities are tightly negotiated, the less space there is for young people to exercise agency, to be grown up autonomous members of society.

Choice by young people doesn't mean that there is no role for the youth worker. Keeping that choice open for young people is a key role. Youth work can seem to operate in clusters of people and resources. Group work theory makes it clear enough that there are groups to be formed (Tuckman) or nurtured (Randall and Southgate), so that they can get on with performing, energising, achieving. The difficulty is the people who join late. Resources, time, money and space get allocated to the group and newcomers are faced with having to choose what others have chosen, or to get nothing. Youth workers are the people who need to let the established group be a bit autonomous and be there to help new choices be made by young people who are not currently making choices. Trying to change the pattern of the week's sessions, or opening up a new group gives most youth workers the sense of how challenging it can be to maintain a commitment to choice by young people.

Youth workers who plan young people's choices can seem to be manipulative, and in what sense can they be free choices? And, what if we end up doing things that are regarded as frivolous or just playing? In the last case the UN Convention explicitly protects children's right to play (Article 31). I comfort myself by comparing the choices I offer young people with those offered by others who work with young people: are they more wide ranging, free, open than colleagues in other agencies. Anne Foreman (1990) encouraged youth workers to plan for unplanned learning outcomes. We are there to make and maintain the space where young people can make their own choices.

Association and social capital

Can we measure association? Can we judge the long term benefits of encouraging association? One metric could be the idea of social capital. Two nations that have persisted in articulating the way society is organised can help our understanding: the USA and France.

De Tocqueville wrote a study of the USA in 1835. He noticed how Americans did not like government, and that when they wanted to change, improve or reinforce something in society they formed associations with others to create a greater impact than acting as individuals (De Tocqueville, 1956, p95). He could see how meetings and speaking in a group made a bigger impact than being on your own and simply writing. LJ Hanifan, in 1916, used 'social capital' to describe: *those tangible substances [that] count for most in the daily lives of people: namely good will, fellowship, sympathy, and social intercourse among the individuals and families who make up a social unit.* It may be that he was spelling out what John Dewey meant in using 'social capital' in *The school and society* in 1899. Pierre Bourdieu (2000) picked up the theme of the contacts, friendships and social links:

> *Social capital is the product of the actual or potential resources available to an individual who has a durable resource of relationships, pretty much in institutional form: knowing other people, or having ways of getting to know others. In other words it is belonging to a group that provides permanent and useful social bonds'*
>
> (My translation from Chauviré 2003, p13)

Most recently Robert Putnam wrote about the collapse of associations in the USA and the loss of social capital in *Bowling alone* (2000) and restarted a discussion that distinguishes bonding capital and bridging capital, neatly capturing the value of the capital from Bourdieu's comments. Bonding capital describes the process of people finding support and reliance in closed groups, such as a ghetto, and takes as a premise that the capital is a way of managing the barriers to wider society. Bridging capital takes individuals beyond their roots and immediate contacts to open up ways of getting to know others who they would otherwise never have met.

The nature of the social capital that is developed by association is important for youth workers. Typically open clubs have been neighbourhood clubs serving the working classes. If association is encouraged uncritically, and without looking at the issue of transforming their social capital, the young people will reinforce their reliance on weak social capital that focuses on the bonds that they already know. If association is addressed as an opportunity to create bridging social capital to improve their life chances (or outcomes) then youth work may be doing more than ensuring that young people have the right to meet. Projects that take this approach intervene in the naturally occurring groups; to mix up boys and girls, black and white; they organise partnerships with other places, exchanges, take part in regional, national and international events, and use widely recognised schemes like the Duke of Edinburgh Award. All these take association on beyond what their families would normally provide.

Review

Let us review four elements that make up association. First, youth work is there to guarantee society's desire for some space in the public domain for young people to meet each other. Second, we do this because it is a right for young people to gather in the same way that it is a, reasonably behaved, adult's right. Third, young people choose to meet up and can see the good in it from their point of view. Fourth, youth workers are there to take an active part in helping the associating go well.

Good youth workers are educated, reflective professionals who have thought through what is likely to happen. Young people in their mid-teens are encountering things for the first time. The adults in a community may be bewildered parents, desperate neighbours, over optimistic or exploitative. Youth workers should be the most capable of thinking through what might happen. Association is about making good boundaries so that young people can meet each other. It is not a surprise that some of the best youth projects have good walls and don't let adults see in. I still admire the detached youth worker in Consett who found ways of dealing with adult anxieties about young people meeting on the streets in a string of settlements, without running around like a wet hen.

But, to return to the beginning, the people who began to create associations in the seventeenth century would ask us: *what is this association for?* They devised associations to develop joint activities and encourage civilised developments that were not possible for individuals. Association developed learning (the Workers' Education Association), knowledge (the Association for the Advancement of Science), or culture (the Football Association). The Albemarle report places association alongside other things: training and challenge, and asked the excellent question *What have they gained from being together? and the only answer can be Nothing or Nothing good.* (Albemarle, 1960, p55) Association is a good thing, but needs to be with other processes. Albemarle made strong links between association and 'counsel' (Albemarle, 1960, p53), and we will look at the supporting values of equality and democratic participation. But like Albemarle we need to look at the learning that happens in youth work too.

Listening

Who listens to young people?

The idea that society listens to young people may seem a little unlikely. Public policy speaks to and about young people. Public figures target, address, describe, caricature, slander, libel, abuse, stigmatise, insult, vilify, pour scorn on, put down, degrade, belittle, and malign young people. There seems no limit to the amount of words that can be aimed and fired at young people. With all that noise from the adults where would we find the quiet to do the listening?

And yet, of all the people who work with young people, youth workers and youth researchers get the chance to listen to what young people have to say. When we listen in disbelief to another bizarre pronouncement it is because it is too strong on the speaking and too weak on the listening. In this section we will unpack and reflect on the way listening helps good things happen for young people and the way in which this is good for wider society.

Listening gives young people the first say

The work starts from where young people are in relation to their own values, views and principles, as well as their own personal and social space.

(National Occupational Standards, 2008, value 2)

Youth work pays attention to young people first of all. Youth work is designed with young people at the heart. The entry requirement is that the young person is a young person, not that they have achieved, or can achieve, or ought to achieve a particular goal. Shildrick and MacDonald report the importance of a voluntary youth work project for a group of 21 year olds: unlike many youth services 'for kids' it welcomed them. It was voluntary, and pre-existing friendship groups were welcomed. They weren't brought together as a set of targeted NEETs (i.e. young people Not in Education Employment or Training, 2008, p51).

Listening for nuance and diversity

Listening to young people we find that different young people need different types of work to respond to the diverse conversations we have. This sounds obvious, but the history of youth work has bad examples of starting from crude assumptions about young people. For example: black young people are expected to make do with what is offered to the dominant white culture (Chauhan, 1989, p36). Girls were assumed not to have specific interests even if they were in the majority (Roberts, 1991). BME (Black and Minority Ethnic people) is meant to: *wrap up the needs, desires and challenges of young men from north, south, west, east and central Africa, the many islands of the Caribbean, most of eastern Europe, Asia, Muslim, Christian, Sikh, gypsy, Irish and every other minority community in England at any given time* (Izekor, 2007, p68). We will return to the issues of equality, but it is worth noting here how the UN Convention makes explicit the areas of children's life that need to be valued as we listen: their identity, opinions, creative expression, freedom of thought and their language (Articles 8,12,13,14,30, and 40). The personal is frankly quite complex and unknown to outsiders if you don't put the time into listening.

Getting to know who the young people are, let alone what they think they'd like to do, is still something where there are significant failings. The issue of Muslim youth work illustrates the point well. The British Muslim population has the youngest age profile of all UK religious groups, about a third are under 16 in 2006, many were living in the Neighbourhood Renewal Areas, where we know that young people are a key concern (Roberts, 2006). And yet youth work is not planned with their needs understood, with the most visible public funding to 'prevent violent extremism'. The need to understand young people properly is the bedrock of good youth work. Without it people are excluded and standard methods are imposed crudely, likely to result in young people choosing not to join in.

Listening for complexity

Social science provides one starting point for listening. Youth Studies researchers investigate analyse and theorise by listening carefully to young people. To do good youth work, we need to keep finding out about the young people in our area. A women's project in Washington goes out regularly to find out who the young women are who are pushing a baby round the shopping centre. Up to date public data allows us to update our community profiles all the time. New developments mean that youth workers need to go out and knock on doors to find out who is living there, even before public data is collected. What we learn at university needs to be taken out into regular youth work if the practice is to be good. Knocking the complexity of what we do is one way of keeping young people in a weak position and youth workers underpaid: *It's not rocket science, youth work.* To which I reply: *No, we can do rocket science. Every month a rocket goes up. Doing good things for young people round here is trickier, that requires real thought.* Keep finding out, keep analysing and assume nothing. Good youth workers are expected to be able to describe the facts and processes of young people's lives in the search for good things to do with them.

Listening as a historic youth work method

Listening to young people has strong practical and theoretical roots in the disciplines close to counselling. 'Counsel' for young people was mentioned in the Albemarle report. The tradition of youth work had grown up that young people in the early part of their working life were often isolated from a conversation with decent civilised adults who were concerned about them being excellent human beings rather than victims of the market or others' abuse.

Maude Stanley provides a case study of an adult explaining the characteristics of young women's lives to the wider, adult population. She was writing this in 1890 to attract support from the wealthy and influential. Her observations are based on careful attention to the lives of the young women.

CASE STUDY

Maude Stanley in 1890 saw the need for clubs for working girls.

How can the working girl find the recreation she must have after ten or eleven hours of monotonous work? Their recreation they find loitering around the streets after dark, when work is over, with some chosen companion . . . sometimes rough play with boys and lads, after a time the walk around; looking in shop windows, attracted by the gas lit stalls. Then comes, according their means, a visit to the music hall, the cheap theatres, the gin palaces, the dancing saloons and the wine shop; then soon follows other temptations, the easy sliding into greater sin, the degradation and downfall of all womanly virtue.

(Booton, 1985, p53)

Girls with a strong sense of honesty are often sorely tried and perplexed with the dishonest habits forced on them by their employers . . . What can a girl do? . . . fraudulent practice is so common that too often the work girl's ideas of honesty get clouded and the whole tone of her moral nature is lowered.

(Booton, 1985, p101)

For Stanley, the youth worker was there to listen to the girl trying to make sense of her life, and to encourage her to stick to her principles.

ACTIVITY 2.3

- *What admirable qualities in the girls' lives does Stanley show that they have?*

- *What social settings look like moral risks?*

- *List the bad things she includes in this passage.*

- *Which of these bad things concern our society today? Why?*

- *Does Stanley begin to make a moral case for a club for these girls?*

Listening as a professional skill

In the twentieth century listening became a highly developed theme in the caring professions. It is not the purpose of this book to prepare you to be an effective listener but insights into listening have deepened good practice with young people. Maud Stanley listened and learnt about the young people she worked with in a general way. Chad Varah and Carl Rogers changed the way listening is done and the value given to it.

Chad Varah was a priest whose first job after ordination in 1935 was *to bury the body of a 14-year-old girl who had killed herself when her menstruation started, not knowing what was 'wrong' with her and having no one she could ask* (Varah, 1985, p19). His first professional response was to find ways to give advice about sex. In 1953 a job in London gave him a base to focus specific work with the suicidal. The idea was that people would ring up an expert and that would stop the suicide attempts. Volunteers came along to help occupy the people who were waiting.

> *What did they say when they attached themselves to some tearful or withdrawn or agitated caller? Their most frequent remarks seemed to be: Mmmmmm. And: How sad. I am sorry. Not to mention: won't you have another cup of coffee? And, when challenged by the caller: No, not at all take your time. No, I've got nothing else to do. Or when asked for advice: I wouldn't know what to advise. I'm not any sort of expert. What do you feel would be best?*

> (Varah, 1985, p24)

The insight of the Samaritans has been that patient listening and human sympathy is good for us.

Carl Rogers also reflected on and developed listening. The key phrase, in terms of behaviour is: unconditional positive regard. Positive regard is what we might call love, affection, showing an interest, making a bond of friendship; the good affectionate bonds that make us flourish. Rogers qualifies that with 'unconditional': you don't need to do something to get the affection; it will still be there for you.

ACTIVITY **2.4**

- Counselling has developed complicated expectations; what do you notice about Varah's description of what the Samaritans do?

- How does Varah's description connect to what many youth workers do in conversation with young people?

- Why is Rogers' approach of 'unconditional positive regard' good?

- Is it the right approach for youth workers? What reasons would you give either way?

Listening and association

The focus on young people choosing to meet and saying what is important to them is at the heart of youth work. Davies and Gibson contrast 'model centred social education', where the adults have a particular agenda, and 'client centred practice' (1967, p134ff). They comment on model-centred social education:

> There is nothing sinister about adults working to recruit others. . . to their own interests or values and to see others following in their footsteps . . . though the benefit derived from the contact of an enthusiastic adult with a willing young person is in a sense unreliable and haphazard, dependent on the accident of their meeting, it frequently means that the young person has an opportunity to undergo an experience which otherwise they would have missed.

> What does seem dubious is that such adults should comprise the staff of what is intended to be a young person's general social club in the district. For then the young person does not get what they bargained for, which was a chance to be sociable, spread their wings, discover their own needs and express choices. Had they gone . . . to a club which said over the door 'amateur dramatics' or 'judo club' they might reasonably expect the staff to have a fairly clear idea about how they wished to spend their time.

> *(1967, p135ff)*

The persistence of youth work based on what is in the adult's head can be seen in Anne Foreman's criticism of 'Youth workers as redcoats'. Youth workers focus on activities and fun that they decide will suit young people's leisure. Managed targets can reinforce this adult driven approach. 'Participation' gets defined simply as counting the number of people taking part (1987, p12ff). I will discuss participation in more detail later, but for the moment let us contrast this adult agenda with the young person's opportunity to form ideas, develop decisions and carry out activities themselves.

Creating 'client centred' youth work requires a thoughtfulness, self consciousness, learning and discipline to separate the adult from their own agenda and dependence on native wit (Davies and Gibson, 1967, p140). This is not just a collection of skills and competences.

> In order to give it direction . . . it needs a set of occupational principles which will show the worker what is indicated by their responsibility to society in general, to clients, and

to themselves as a mature, independent human being. (The youth worker) must fashion something comparable with the occupational principles which circumscribe a doctor's freedom of action and indicate their ethical responsibilities. The principles need to be sought deliberately and articulated explicitly.

(Davies and Gibson, 1967, p143)

They argue that such a framework cannot be established by an academic process carried on between individuals with no day to day knowledge of work with young people, the actual relationships, and the particular pressures of society. It cannot be made up from a collection of *abstract concepts and theoretical ideas* (Davies and Gibson, 1967). The values listed in the National Occupational Standards (2008) and the ethical principles (NYA, 1999) respond to the specific search described here. But the important element here is that listening expresses a disposition, an attitude of the professional youth worker to attend to the interests of the young person first.

Review: listening

Let us review the key points about listening to young people. First, listening is essential to determine who we are working with. Second, it gives us nuanced detail which it is our duty to know both for our work and for the way in which we might interpret young people's lives to wider society. Third, listening builds trust, providing healing and safety for young people. Finally it characterises a youth work that is there to benefit young people who take part in it. Listening is the means by which youth workers find out what to do, build their work with young people, and guarantee that their primary focus is on young people. Listening is a key part of learning. As advocates of learning for change youth workers can model the saying: 'listen and learn'.

ACTIVITY **2.5**

- *Identify the key features of association.*

- *What are the behaviours of youth workers that will help association?*

- *Why is it good for young people to have youth workers who are listeners?*

- *Explain how each theme links to the ethical codes.*

- *Analyse the wider benefits for society of these youth work themes.*

C H A P T E R   R E V I E W

Youth work expresses values about people in our society. We assert that young people should be able to meet together and decide what to do just as adults do in democratic life. The transitional nature of young people's lives justifies specific professionals facilitating this association. Listening is a primary activity for youth workers: it puts young people centre stage, allows for nuanced understanding, enables power to be exercised by young people and can have therapeutic results. Both association and listening are themes that recur throughout the historical practice of youth work reflecting their effectiveness and importance.

Batsleer, J (2008) *Informal learning in youth work*. London: Sage. Addresses listening, pp63–68.

Jacobs, M (2000) *Swift to hear*. London: Library of Pastoral Care. Includes excellent exercises to improve your listening skills.

Jeffs, T and Smith, M (2005) *Informal education*. Nottingham: Education Heretics Press. Some excellent reading in chapters 2 (listening) and 3 (Association) with good follow up exercises.

Albemarle Report (1960) *The youth service in England and Wales*. London: HMSO.

Booton, F (1985) *Studies in social education 1860–1890*. Hove: Benfield Press.

Bourdieu, P (2000) *Les structures socials de l'economie*. Paris: Seuil.

Chauhan, V (1989) *Beyond steel bands and samosas*. Leicester: National Youth Bureau.

Chauviré ,C and Fontaine, O (2003) *Le vocabulaire de Bourdieu*. Paris: Ellipses.

Cohen, S (1972 /2002) *Folk devils and moral panics*, London; Routledge.

Davies, B and Gibson, A (1967) *The social education of the adolescent*. London: University of London Press.

De Tocqueville, A. (1956) *Democracy in America*. New York: Penguin.

Dewey, J (1899) *The school and society*. Chicago: University of Chicago Press (available online).

Education and Inspections Act 2006 The full Act is available on the internet at www.opsi.gov.uk/ACTS/acts2006/ukpga_20060040_en_2#pt1-l1g6

Flavell, J. (1968) *The development of role taking and communication skills in children*. New York: John Wiley and Sons.

Foreman, A (1990) Personality and the curriculum, in Jeffs, T and Smith, M, *Using informal education*. Basingstoke: Open University Press and online at www.infed.org

Handy, C (1985) *Understanding organisations*. London: Penguin.

Hanifan, L.J (1916) The rural school community center. *Annals of the American Academy of Political and Social Science* 67: 130–138.

Izekor, J (2007) Challenging the stereotypes, in Sallah, M and Howson, C, *Working with black young people*. Lyme Regis: Russell House Publishing.

MacDonald, R and Marsh, J (2005) *Disconnected youth*. Basingstoke: Palgrave Macmillan.

Mayhew, H (1985) *London Labour and the London poor*. London: Penguin.

Niebuhr, R (1932) *Moral man and immoral society*. New York: Scribner.

NOS (2008) *National and professional occupational standards for youth work*. London: LLUK.

NYA (2005) Ethical conduct in youth work, in Harrison, R and Wise, C, *Working with young people.* London: Sage.

Putnam, R (2000) *Bowling alone: the collapse and revival of American community.* New York: Simon and Schuster.

Randall, R and Southgate, J (1980) *Cooperative and community group dynamics.* London: Barefoot Books.

Rawls, J (1971) *A theory of justice.* Cambridge, MA: Belknap Press.

Reed, B (1978) *The dynamics of religion.* London: Darton Longman Todd.

Roberts, J (1991) Two girls for every boy. *Youth and Policy,* 35: 8–13.

Roberts, J (2006) Making a place for Muslim youth work in British youth work. *Youth and Policy,* 92: 19–31

Rutter, M. *et al.* (1979) *15000 Hours.* London: Open Books.

Shildrick, T and MacDonald, R (2008) Understanding youth exclusion: critical moments, social networks and social capital. *Youth and Policy,* 99: 43–54.

Tuckman, B (1965) Developmental sequence in small groups. *Psychological Bulletin,* 63: 384–399.

Varah, C (1985) *The Samaritans.* London: Constable.

Chapter 3
Values: equality

In this chapter I will explore a youth work value that express society's desire to have good things happen for young people. Youth work tries to do something good by creating an understanding and a practice of equality among the young people we work with. Why do we do this?

Promoting equality and fairness is protected and resourced to make our democratic society assume the character of interaction between individuals and groups that we have decided is good. Treating people equally and taking part in public decisions are adult interactions in the public sphere and our society values, protects, and encourages them. Equality and participation (Chapter 4) are contested by many in our society and young people find themselves caught up in the debate. It is certainly the case that people choose in their private lives not to carry out equality legislation, or, not to vote, or, not to take part in political decision making. In this chapter we will see how society sets a moral agenda to ensure equality for all and youth work is a space to experience and develop this value. By the end of this chapter you should be able to:

• define equality accurately;

• identify and evaluate ways in which societies express a commitment to equality;

• explain how equality is organised in daily youth work.

Links to the National and Professional Occupational Standards for Youth Work 2008

Values	Principle activity area	Examples of Units
Equality of opportunity:	2. Promote equality and young people's interests and welfare	1.1.2, 1.3.2, 1.3.3, 2.3.1, 2.3.2, 2.3.3, 2.4.1, 2.4.2

Defining equality

Here are four definitions of equality. The different meanings need to be used carefully because they can be used to undermine arguments about equality.

Equality is:

1 the condition of being equal in quantity, amount, value, intensity, in maths, an exact correspondence;

2 the condition of being equal in dignity, privileges, power with others;

3 fairness, impartiality, equity;

4 evenness, uniformity.

(Shorter Oxford English Dictionary, 1975)

Definition 1 is about the operation of maths and we are dealing with people so this needs using with care. This definition may support the two dominant meanings we will use: here are two examples. We can tell if women are given equal dignity at work (definition 2) by calculating if their pay is equal to men's pay. We know if a youth service is offered fairly (definition 3) to the black community by calculating comparable intensity of use per 1000 of the ethnic groups. Note especially that the values in definition 1 are numerical on a scale, not ethical values, which are what we are interested in.

Definitions 2 and 3 are the dominant definitions for our ethics. Definition 2 focuses on lived experience of each person: do they have equal dignity, privileges, and power? We use this definition to evaluate human rights in a state. Do they have equal rights, an equal entitlement? We ask the same questions in youth work. Does each young person get the same level of respect?

Definition 3 focuses on the behaviour of people who organise and make a difference to others. It can be used to evaluate systems of government. We evaluate our practice as youth work professionals. Do we behave fairly, with impartiality, toward young people? When we look at our behaviour we notice the inequality that young people experience under definition 2 and behave in ways that facilitate greater equality. So, in youth work equality means creating both inclusive and redistributive opportunities.

Definition 4 is less helpful and can be used mischievously to undermine arguments and practice promoting equality. Unlike this definition, you know that people are not the same: they differ in physical, mental, spiritual, and social characteristics. Each person wants to choose a path for their lives. It is the purpose of youth work to include the full range so that each young person can experience equal rights (definition 2) and so that our practice is fair (definition 3).

Equality in West Wheatley

A voluntary group is set up by a white middle-aged man in a village that is almost entirely white. The three families at the village shop, the take-away and doctor's surgery are the exceptions to the white population who have lived here for years. The youth group meets in West Wheatley village hall that only receives indirect funding from the council in small grants. The youth leader keeps the group white and encourages traditional roles between the boys and girls that come. He excluded one young person for talking in a positive way about gay celebrities.

He says that the group reflects the 'white highlands' area it is in and most of the girls want to bake and cheerlead for the boys' team games.

- *What is wrong with this group?*

- *Why is it wrong?*

- *Which definition of equality does the worker seem to be using?*

- *How is the young people's development being hindered?*

- *What aspects of equality (2), as the young people's rights, are being prevented?*

- *Describe how the commitment to equality (3), as the youth worker being fair, is being ignored.*

Equality in society: a wider context

Who rules and who benefits?

Achieving a combination of equal entitlement for each person (definition 2), and fair government by the state (definition 3) has been the heart of many debates and revolutions since the Athenians first proposed democracy as opposed to monarchy. Democracy continues to have its critics and one of its best defences is to consider the alternative systems of rule. The table shows the 12 different systems.

In real life several systems often work together. The separate names allow us to analyse the arrangements of power systems that need to be challenged. For instance England in 1750 combined six of these systems.

1 George II was king: it was a monarchy.

2 The Whigs controlled the British Parliament as an oligarchy, reinforced by 'rotten boroughs' (see Blackadder) and the hereditary House of Lords.

3 The African slave trade made Britain rich: apartheid.

4 Women could not inherit or act in public as men could: patriarchy.

5 Landowners could use their financial position to 'enclose' common land and waters as their private property for agriculture and field sports: capitalism.

6 The Church of England reinforced the status quo by defining who took part in law and government, benefiting from tithes, glebe and mineral rights: theocracy.

7 Apart perhaps from Bath, where rich invalids went for a cure, impairments ensured a restricted social role: social disability.

Twelve alternatives to democracy

Name of the system	Entitlement for each person	Form of government
Monarchy	One family is superior to all others and relationships to that family determine status.	The same family always decides.
Matriarchy	Is determined by what a woman chooses.	Mam, or Nana, decides.
Patriarchy	Is determined by what men choose.	We do what suits the man.
Apartheid	Is determined by a ranking of people according to a constructed system of racial separation.	We let the top, racially defined, group determine the important decisions and manage the key resources.
Oligarchy	Inside the small group (often defined by wealth): much power; outside: little.	A small group decide everything.
Dictatorship	Relation to the key individual gives status.	One person decides according to their own criteria.
Capitalism	Freedoms increase according to their ability to control the money they can invest or spend.	Permits and protects the investment of spare money in projects designed to make more money.
Tyranny	Related to the ability and willingness to frighten or be frightened.	Decision making is rooted in violence and fear designed to secure control.
Heptarchy	Each royal family is superior to all other families and relationships to that family determine status.	Seven kings ruling an area independently.
Anarchy	Unclear. Each asserts individual dignity.	No one is in charge and there is no system of government and social organisation.
Theocracy	Depends on a relationship to the key religious organisation.	We do what people tell us they think God wants.
Social disability	The 'able bodied' have access to all areas. Those defined by medical conditions or physical impairments are infantilised or denied full entitlement.	The 'able bodied' are in charge and set restrictions for those defined by medical conditions or physical impairments.

Applying the systems to experience

Working as a group: share out the 12 different systems and answer the following questions for each. Feedback your ideas to the whole group.

• *What experience at neighbourhood level do you have of this type of government?*

• *Research other historical examples that fit your type of government.*

Equality in USA and France

Two nations have persistently sought to practise and develop equality in the way in which government has been exercised and citizen's rights protected: the USA and France. Their written and practical expressions of equality have had a much wider impact through the impact of their political power and the alliances which the UK, at least, have had with both. They influenced each other, and drew on British reflections on government and in turn contributed to the United Nations where their local arrangements were blended as a beginning of international democratic law. In this book you will find out more about the UN Convention on the Rights of the Child.

Equality in the USA

The 1776 Declaration of Independence balanced the equality of all and the rights of each person, with the role of government:

> *We hold these truths to be self evident, that all men are created equal, that they are endowed by their creator with certain unalienable rights, that among these are life, liberty and the pursuit of happiness. That to secure these rights governments are instituted among men deriving their just powers from the consent of the governed.*
>
> (Commager, 1982, p95)

The declaration rejected the governance of the King George III of Great Britain and, among other things, accused him of 'absolute Despotism' preventing the rule of law and representative government. Constitutions, laws and a Bill of Rights were developed for States and the United States to express this equality of power and dignity of person.

It was by no means complete equality and the history of the USA can in part be told as a widening of the understanding and practice of equality. The Civil War was fought about the possibility that there should be no more slavery. A century later the civil rights movement expressed the need to improve the full and complete citizenship of the black US population. Lincoln captured the contested nature of equality in a few remarks at Gettysburg:

> *Four score and seven years ago our fathers brought forth upon this continent a new nation, conceived in liberty and dedicated to the proposition that all men are created equal. Now we are engaged in a great civil war, testing whether that nation can long endure.*
>
> (Lincoln, 1907, p213)

He also used a deceptively simple phrase to express the equality of power, commitment, and service required for equality to flourish: . . . *that government of the people, by the people, for the people, shall not perish from the earth* (Lincoln, 1907, p214).

Equality in France

The 1789 Declaration of the Rights of Man in France did not restrict its statements to France alone, using the adjective 'Français' once only to define the source of the universal rights. Article 1 states: *Man is born and remains free and equal in law* (Pecheul, 2001, p18). The purpose, as in the USA, was to end monarchy. But the Declaration also sought to overcome the powers of the nobility (oligarchy), and the clergy (theocracy), who contributed to the unequal power and status. The three values of the secular state were expressed in Robespierre's motto: Liberté, Égalité, Fraternité. The vigorous military and legislative activity of Napoleon took the cause of the revolution and its quest for equality to different parts of Europe and the French Empire.

The contested nature of equality can be seen in France too: changes of government by internal political change and external military defeat meant that they reworked the old commitments in new constitutions. In 1848 it looked cautious: the republic is based on: *the family, work, property and public order* (Pecheul, 2001, p27). After the Occupation the 1946 Constitution: Article 1, specifically contrasts the freedom of the United Nations with the enslaving and degrading behaviour of the defeated regime towards humanity (Pecheul, 2001, p48). Article 3 states plainly an extension of equality: *the law guarantees to all women, in all domains, equal rights with men* (Pecheul, 2001, p49).

Full equality is a continuing debate (see Chapter 9) but both French and American debates have helped change how we express and understand human rights. The development of UN agreements, and international law, has become part of the UK legal system both by treaty and by statute.

Inequality in Europe

Overcoming oligarchies that were able to wield power because of their social or financial status meant that seeking 'the greatest good for the greatest number' was a theme of nineteenth-century Utilitarians. Universal suffrage, everyone voting, would surely produce fair results. Large numbers can create majorities but they don't necessarily achieve social equality. One of the downsides of majorities is that they can behave badly to minority groups. Germans still debate if Hitler gained power by a majority vote. How many actually voted? Remember the level of physical intimidation used against voters. The regime seems to have combined dictatorship, oligarchy, and, above all, tyranny. The Nazi regime is a vivid example of how a majority can use its power to attack minorities: Jews, homosexuals, Sinti, Roma, the mentally ill, Trade Unionists, communists. That regime also has the potential to bequeath us their labels to divide humanity (*Time Out*, 2006, p82). Reflecting on the experience of the Nazi period Martin Niemöller drew attention to the need to recognise common humanity and not to be attached to identity labels that separate.

> *In Germany they first came for the Communists,*
> *and I didn't speak up because I wasn't a Communist.*
> *Then they came for the Jews,*
> *and I didn't speak up because I wasn't a Jew.*

Then they came for the trade unionists,
and I didn't speak up because I wasn't a trade unionist.
Then they came for the Catholics,
and I didn't speak up because I was a Protestant.
Then they came for me —
and by that time no one was left to speak up.

(Niemoller, 1959)

Detailed, explicit statements of the equalities we expect and the rights to which we are entitled are, in part, a legacy of dealing with the Nazi regime.

Rawls: thinking about equality

John Rawls' Theory of Justice argues for equality as a development of justice as fairness in the social contract ideas of Locke, Rousseau and Kant (Rawls, 1971, p11). Rawls' advantage over these philosophers is that he has seen and heard the debates since the eighteenth century, and writes as civil rights movements are active in the USA, France and Ireland (*see* his sections on civil disobedience 1971, pp371–391). The problem is that liberty clashes with equality. Freedom allows people to snowball money (*see* his reference to Keynes 1971, p298ff), property and influence as a power that can control roles and associations in unequal ways that further enlarge their snowball of status.

Rawls imagines setting rules at the start of society. What would the rules of association (see Chapter 2) look like? He develops an argument based on justice for all. His proposal relates to real life. As we will see, new equality laws develop an equal society by addressing specific inequality and stating underpinning rights.

Rawls argues for two principles, two priority rules and a general concept of equality.

1 First Principle: Each person is to have an equal right to the most extensive total system of equal basic liberties compatible with a similar system of liberty for all (Rawls, 1971, p250).

2 Second Principle: social and economic inequalities are to be arranged so that they are both:

- to the greatest benefit of the least advantaged;

- attached to offices and positions open to all under conditions of fair equality of opportunity (1971, p302).

3 First priority rule: if liberty is restricted then this can only be for the sake of liberty:

- less extensive liberty will give everyone more liberty, (the right to roam over land owned for grazing would meet this rule);

- a less than equal liberty must be acceptable to those with lesser liberty.

4 Second priority rule: justice is more important than efficiency or the greatest good for the greatest number and fair opportunity is more important than difference.

5 Any inequality of opportunity must enhance the opportunity of those with the lesser opportunity, (a contribution to the debate about positive action);

6 An excessive rate of saving must on balance mitigate the burden of those bearing this hardship.

All social primary goods – liberty (*see* Rawls, 1971, p61) and opportunity, income and wealth, and the bases of self respect are to be distributed equally unless an unequal distribution of any or all is to the advantage of the least favoured (Rawls, 1971, p303).

There are three impacts of equality.

1 Equality in an institution. Justice operates as regularity. Everyone gets the same treatment (Rawls, 1971, p504).

2 The structural equality of the institution. Justice allows all to take part. All can join and have the same rights to each role (Rawls, 1971, p505).

3 Entitlement to equality is based on the capacity for moral personality. That means that natural attributes are not used to judge (Rawls, 1971, p507).

Like children's rights capacity, not realisation, is sufficient for the entitlement (Rawls, 1971, p509).

ACTIVITY **3.2**

Prepare answers to and then discuss the following:

• *identify when rules of association are set at the beginning in youth work;*

• *how do your experiences show the importance of Rawls' first principle in youth work?*

• *give examples of the fair operation of Rawls' second principle in youth work;*

• *how can you apply the first priority rule to managing behaviour in youth work?*

• *explain why equality depends upon justice.*

Equality in England and Wales: introduction

The UK has no written constitution – unlike the countries that have spelled out how they wish society to develop. Nor did the Nazis occupy it – unlike those countries like France (or Germany) who have redefined their commitment to human rights since 1945. Nonetheless, it has been a source of equality practice. Both the Americans and French referred to English sources: Blackstone, the Civil Wars of 1642–1649, Hobbes' Leviathan of 1651 and John Locke's social contract. I will discuss how our society debates equality. I will list some of the laws to create greater equality in the UK with brief descriptions of the powers created by that law. You will look at equality in general and then themes of gender, race, disability and sexuality.

Equality in general in the UK

People seeking greater equality is a sign that there are imbalances of power. We can see this at times when one part of society looks on while important decisions are made by the powerful. This is not just a recent concern. On 29 October 1647 victorious Parliamentarians discussed how England should be governed. It was the second day of the Putney debates. They were arguing about who should be able to vote in elections. Colonel Thomas Rainborough challenged the idea that only the propertied class should decide:

> I desired that those that had engaged in it [the fight against the King] might be included. For really I think that the poorest he that is in England has a life to live, as the greatest he; and therefore truly, sir, I think it's clear, that every man that is to live under a government ought first by his own consent to put himself under that government; and I do think that the poorest man in England is not at all bound in a strict sense to that government that he has not had a voice to put himself under. . .

(Robertson, 2007, p69)

All those over 21, men and women, could only vote after 1928. This inclusion of all adults allows decisions to be made on the basis of what most people think. Majority decisions are good because they allow us to avoid a special interest group (oligarchy), or person telling us what to do (monarchy, theocracy or dictatorship). That sort of discussion and decision making that includes us all is called democracy. Democracy is good because it values conversation, debate and peaceful decision making that can include everyone. Respecting and protecting difference in people is what we seek now. Current legislation tries to be a unity offering equality to all under the law: which is why there is a single Equality Commission. Recent legislation includes:

Equality Act 2006

- A single Commission for Equality and Human Rights.

- Duty on the public sector to promote equality between women and men.

- Access to good facilities and services without discrimination based on religion or belief.

Employment Equality (Age) Regulation 2006

- Stops age discrimination in employment and vocational training.

Gender

Achieving equality of rights for women has been a long campaign. The Fawcett Society (founded 1866) is still hard at work with abiding issues, such as equal pay. Women and men make up roughly half of the population each, so it makes no sense to talk about women as a minority. The legislation since 1970 has tried to address the scandal of inequality of adult life chances for women. These campaigns have attracted wide debate because they affect so many people and settings. For youth work there have been related campaigns about pay and roles for male and female youth workers, suitable provision and impact on girls and boys in equal measure; and these debates are still alive with practical consequences. Recent legislation includes:

Equal Pay Act 1970 (Amended)

- Each person has a right to the same contractual pay and benefits as someone of the opposite sex in the same employment.

Sex Discrimination Act 1975

- The Act makes sex discrimination unlawful in employment, education, advertising or when providing housing, goods, services or facilities.

- It is unlawful to discriminate because someone is married.

The Employment Equality (Sex Discrimination) Regulations 2005

- Adds indirect discrimination and harassment.

- Prohibits discrimination on the grounds of pregnancy or maternity leave.

- Sets out the extent to which it is discriminatory to pay a woman less than she would otherwise have been paid due to pregnancy or maternity issues.

CASE STUDY

Equality is about changing the agenda

I used to work across a large area, supporting separate church groups. I had no way of choosing which young people I worked with as they were already members of a group. I suspected that I was working with a larger number of girls than boys but was not sure. I started keeping a tally and built up records that showed that I saw 'two girls for every boy'.

The heart of the work I was doing was the personal, social and spiritual development of the young people. Quite often this was based on the bible readings set for the day or the week. Characteristically, these readings had been chosen long ago by groups of mainly men, based on ancient patterns of readings usually chosen exclusively by men. Stories focused on men being called by God. Men chose what to do with their lives. Men were eloquent or heroic or faced suffering to be saved. It was all very unsuitable for groups of mainly women. I began to use stories about women and was delighted to watch the engagement and development of the young women who identified with their experiences. The materials fitted well into the contemporary development of women's ministry in the 1990s.

(Roberts, 1991)

Race

We have legislation responding to discrimination based on race because black and white activists want to end the offensive treatment of the black community. Systematic exclusion from employment, good pay, education, effective justice, containment within limited roles and opportunities; these all needed challenging by the law. The 'heartfelt plea': *Please treat us with respect* was heard at the heart of national debate (Macpherson, 1999, p312). A minority in the population, almost unknown to some parts of the country has specific legal remedies and support. In youth work, black workers and the groups used by black young people have been an important part of youth work's history; trying to push the barriers of exclusion out of the young people's way. Recent legislation includes:

Race Relations Act 1976

- Prohibits discrimination on racial grounds in employment, education, and the provision of goods, facilities, services and premises.

Race Relations Amendment Act 2000

- A duty on all public bodies to promote equal opportunity, eliminate racial discrimination and promote good relations between different racial groups.

Race Relations Act 1976 (Amendment) Regulation 2003

New definitions of:

- indirect discrimination and harassment;
- burden of proof requirements;
- continuing protection after employment ceases;
- exemption for a determinate job requirement;
- removal of certain exemptions.

Employment Equality (Religion or Belief) Regulation 2003

- Protects against discrimination on the grounds of religion and belief in employment, vocational training, promotion and working conditions.

Racial and Religious Hatred Act 2006

- People must not intentionally use threatening words or behaviour to stir up hatred against somebody because of what they believe.

Disability

Disability groups have a long history. The development of rights based thinking led to some of those groups seeing the connections between the rights given in law to specific groups and the impact of society on those with impairments. Society can take an impairment and disable the way a person's life turns out. The legislation also allows society to remove barriers for this minority of its members. When we discussed ways of creating inclusive, 'integrated' schools in Sunderland we began with the signature of the Secretary of State for Education, David Blunkett, sent to boarding school from the age of eight because he was blind. Youth work has, at its best, devised projects to enable young people with different abilities to do things together and build up long term relationships. Recent legislation includes:

Disability Discrimination Act 1995

- Outlaws the discrimination of disabled people in employment, provision of goods, and services.

Disability Discrimination Amendment Act 2005

- A duty on public bodies to promote equality for disabled people.

Sexuality

Discrimination on the basis of sexuality has proved difficult to agree on. The very personal and intimate nature of sexuality makes it a difficult subject to debate. Lord Devlin speaking in 1958 identified behaviours that the public would regard as so immoral that they need to be managed by the law. Public reaction would be *intolerance, indignation and disgust* (1965). However, over the years, we have accepted Hart's argument against this position of moral popularism. We live with *a number of mutually tolerant moralities* (Hart, 1963, p63). This is expressed in extending to gay couples the same rights enjoyed in law as heterosexual couples, accepting that heterosexuals are as likely to 'corrupt youth', and so on. For youth work the delicate development of self understanding by each young person includes their sexual responses and personal preferences. The nightmare days when it was illegal because of explicit legislation, aimed at gay citizens and their supporters, to discuss all possibilities are fortunately over. At the heart of this debate is the willingness to respect the young people for themselves, before our adult agenda. Recent legislation includes:

The Sex Discrimination (Gender Reassignment) Regulations 1999

- Prevents sex discrimination relating to gender reassignment, clarifying the law for transsexual people in relation to equal pay and treatment in employment and training.

Employment Equality (Sexual Orientation) Regulation 2003

- Protects against discrimination on the grounds of sexual orientation in employment, vocational training, promotion, and working conditions.

Civil Partnerships Act 2004

- Provides legal recognition and parity of treatment for same-sex couples and married couples, including employment benefits and pension rights.

Gender Recognition Act 2004

- Provides transsexual people with legal recognition in their acquired gender, following from the issue of a full gender recognition certificate by a panel.

Equality Act (Sexual Orientation) Regulations 2007

- Builds on the Equality Act 2006 to protect against discrimination on the grounds of sexual orientation (perceived or actual): in the provision of goods, facilities, services, education; use of premises; in the exercise of public duties.

ACTIVITY 3.3

Focusing on the equality laws

- *Which of these laws make an impact on the youth work you have experienced?*

- *Which of these laws do you wish to find out more about? (**www.opsi.gov.uk/acts.htm**)*

- *What aspects of the legislation surprise you?*

- *What is good about the legislation?*

Equality in work with young people

Laws show us where a society sets its standards. However, legislation is limited. Explicit legal provisions apply to people at work, or trying to work. The law needs formal litigation to bring equality alive. Youth work happens informally in groups that young people choose to join. Youth workers would not want to take young people to court as the first step in developing equality. We need to look at other ways to promote equal rights and fair treatment in youth work. I will explore four areas where youth workers need to be active for equality to be a reality for young people. They are ground rules, group work, keeping an eye on the wider context and planning informal learning.

Negotiating ground rules

Just as law defines acceptable behaviour in wider society, the habit of agreeing ground rules within a group allows young people to define and negotiate the basis of group life. Putting possible behaviours into words moves the child beyond the norms of their family to becoming independent moral agents in society (Piaget, 1977). I will return to the moral development of the child in Chapter 5. Here, we are looking at how we avoid oppressive behaviour and encourage the value of equality. The young person has the chance to make rules that give equal rights to each group member. They wrestle with the problem of how the group behaves fairly. They use Rawls' veil of ignorance (1971, p36) and develop Kant's categorical imperative (1997, p43). Negotiation is a key aspect of making ground rules. If you prepare a laminated sheet the young people don't put the central themes in their own words, or experience the power differences. Persuading other people of the importance of commitment to equality is a social skill that you are developing by studying to be a professional youth worker. Begin with individual preparation, and paired discussion before having a whole group discussion. Encourage a good discussion of the ground rules to clarify what the group agrees.

ACTIVITY 3.4

- *Devise six open questions that will help a group prepare suggestions for ground rules (include themes from legislation).*

- *Compare your questions with those prepared by others.*

- *Improve your questions with their ideas.*

Group work

Effective group work is at the heart of much youth work. We show our commitment to equality in the distinctive, inclusive, and anti-oppressive life of our groups. Close scrutiny of what is actually going on in a group is a core activity of the professional youth worker. Thorough analysis using group theory can unpick the causes of exclusion and inequality.

ACTIVITY 3.5

Using WR Bion to analyse practice and ensure equality.

Bion defines a healthy group when it:

1. *has a common purpose;*

2. *knows where its boundaries lie;*

3. *can absorb new members and lose others without loss of group individuality;*

4. *is free from sub group;*

5. *can cope with discontent;*

6. *has at least three members.*

(Bion, 1991, p25ff)

Apply Bion's themes to a group you work with.

1. *Purpose:*

- *have we a purpose that is agreed and inclusive?*

- *can you write a mission statement to give a clear focus?*

- *is the purpose open enough to achieve equality?*

- *when do you revisit such statements with the group?*

- *what improvements do members suggest?*

2. *Boundaries:*

- *where do the boundaries lie?*

- *who is in and who is out?*

- *equality does not require infinite boundaries. How does your boundary help equality?*

- *Scouts agreed to have girls in their groups. Girlguiding choose to keep their organisation only for girls. What are the benefits of each boundary?*

3. *Changing members:*

- *is it easy for all newcomers to join?*

- *how do we recruit and welcome new members?*

- *do new members have new ideas?*

- *do new members need induction to understand the mission statement?*

- *how do we say goodbye to those leaving?*

4. *Sub groups:*

- *what do we do to avoid or overcome sub groups?*

ACTIVITY **3.5** *continued*

- *do we make it easy for a lads' group to thrive?*

- *do we have a set of ground rules?*

5. *Discontent:*

- *how do we cope with discontent?*

- *what do we do when someone feels excluded?*

- *what do we do when you notice someone eased out?*

6. *Do a couple of young people form most of the youth work you do?*

Keeping an eye on the wider patterns in society

Scrutinising what is going on for young people in their social context is a core activity of the professional youth worker. Close proximity to the lived reality of young people, professional opportunity, and professional education can make strong links between youth work and youth studies. Youth workers are often the people who are best able to articulate what is happening in young people's lives. Youth workers can also respond more quickly than some of the larger more complex state bodies and, by so doing, gain deeper understanding of a new social pattern. Here I give three examples of wider patterns revealed by youth studies.

Demographic change

Changing patterns of population raise difficult questions about the location and sufficiency of youth work resources. The proportions of young people, and older people, change through time and present different patterns of need and anxiety. The Albemarle Report (1960) anticipated the arrival of the 'bulge' of baby boomers as teenagers, accentuated by the ending of National Service. This group's wider impact on society was seen later in the same decade. The youth service complained in the 1950s that they hadn't the resources for this larger group. Albemarle meant that money was spent, staff developed, and buildings dedicated to youth work. These extra resources were in part to address the sense of inequality of provision for those who were leaving school for work at a time when other young people were staying on and progressing to the expanded HE provision.

Close scrutiny of the population and the practice of youth work can reveal specific gaps. The 1967 Hunt Report raised the issue of provision for the young black British population; we might say that the stronger statements of the Thompson Report (1982) reflected the failure to include in British society on an equal basis expressed in the Brixton riots of 1981. Both reports raised the profile and competence of black youth work practice. The current debate about how to provide sufficient Muslim youth work is happening, after a bulge in the number of young 'Muslims' in the population.

The examples show that we improve equality for young people when we look at the bigger picture of the current and anticipated pattern of population, rather than assuming existing provision is sufficient. As population profiles have changed, youth workers show their commitment to equality by presenting the up to date characteristics of need.

Young people's contrasting transitions

We see quite dramatic contrasts in relation to young people's transitions, particularly in education and work. In a group I worked with young people left to go to Russell Group university courses and others to training schemes for the unemployed. Friends from neighbourhoods find themselves separated at their entry into adult life. While we were in the youth group we enjoyed the diversity, built up the interdependence, and sought to achieve a space where equity could be experienced. But the young people's destinations can reinforce the sense of social exclusion and fragmentation. Williamson's interesting study of the 'Milltown Boys revisited' distinguished three broad groups separated by work, possessions and life style, with six young men 'beyond' the lowest classification (Williamson, 2004, p237). As we move between the safe space of our youth work and the world outside where 14–15 per cent of Muslims are unemployed compared with 4 per cent for Christians (National Statistics, 2006) the contrasts raise the moral question: How effective are we at achieving equal chances for the young people we work with? What would we do differently to improve life chances?

Young people and class

This debate raises the wider question of the class position of youth work. The Albemarle report was clear that the youth service was to benefit the large majority who did not continue in full time education (1960, p22). The argument is made in plain moral terms:

> *is it right that this social provision should end so abruptly for the less intellectual, simply because they have been withdrawn from formal education? One can contrast the standard of premises usual in . . . the youth service with those of a residential hostel or undergraduates' common room in almost any redbrick university. . . or of the new secondary modern schools. . . Anyone who has experienced the atmosphere of this type. . . must regret the comparative poverty of social and communal provision for boys and girls who thereafter go immediately into working life. . . If these informal activities are needed by those up to 21 (so long as they are in full time education) they are undoubtedly needed by all those whose intellectual equipment has not been sufficient to keep them under the comfortable umbrella of full time education.*
>
> *(Albemarle Report, 1960, p35ff)*

The moral argument was well enough made then to build some youth centres still in use. The question remains about our society's current willingness to invest enough money in the personal and social development of the 50–60 per cent of young people who do not go into HE.

ACTIVITY 3.6

Discuss the suitability of a range of youth provision in your area, such as: youth shelters, sports facilities, youth centres, and church halls.

Transformation or transmission? The past and youth work

The history of youth work shows different approaches to equality. Some workers led the development of new ways of behaving in society. Youth work was a setting where black leaders found their first opportunities for bringing about change; women workers developed girls' groups to challenge male models of practice. Such workers agreed with Henry Giroux in seeing the learning opportunities of youth work as sites of cultural production and transformation.

Other workers saw their youth work as being the transmission of cultural treasures to the next generation. Derek Tasker (1960) wrote a training programme for young people in Anglican parishes linking case studies to the traditional Biblical material associated with marriage. It is arguable that other youth work was also interested in the reproduction of existing cultural patterns. Did the early YMCA try to create the close supportive community life of a village in urban settings? Did the uniformed organisations try to impose the patterns of authority of the armed forces on youth work?

The ambiguous character of youth work can be seen in the arguments about scouting. Michael Rosenthal (1986) raises uncomfortable arguments about racism in Baden-Powell that sits oddly with a movement that builds bonds of peace across the world. Tim Jeal's biography of Baden-Powell (1989) weighs the historical detail: showing Baden-Powell as a man of his time, and put in the position of depending on, and wishing to decorate black fighters (1989, p284). Elleke Boehmer, in the introduction to the Oxford edition of Scouting for Boys, shows us the nuances in the foundation text. It is a product of Empire (2004, xviii), the Avant-Garde Movement (2004, xxiv), and Modernism (2004, xxxv).

What can we conclude about the past? In many ways youth work reflected the society that produced it. Youth work in the past was ambiguous about equality: the progressives and liberals did one thing, more traditional work did another.

Youth work now

Youth work now is in a less ambiguous position about equality. We live in a society that codifies its statements about equality in law. Money follows work conforming to these codes. The young people we work with are moving from their private family settings to the wider society via our youth work. They need, in various ways, to be prepared for that society; its practices, its rules and the behaviours that will best meet the high ambitions of the legislation. By transforming their experiences of equality we are transmitting the best aspects of our wider society.

Youth work doesn't just fit in with generic legislation. There is an explicit equality for children and young people. The UN Convention on the Rights of the Child applies to those under 18. Article 2 sets a high bar for inclusive youth work. When we use the words for a youth project it reads:

> *We shall respect and ensure the rights set forth in the UN Convention to each child without discrimination of any kind, irrespective of the child's or his or her parent's or legal guardian's race, colour, sex, language, religion, political or other opinion, national, ethnic or social origin, property, disability, birth or other status.*

> *We shall ensure that the child is protected against all forms of discrimination or punishment on the basis of the status, activities, expressed opinions, or beliefs of the child's parents, legal guardians, or family members.*

Ensuring learning to develop an actively equal society

The 2006 Education and Inspections Act empowers youth work to encourage the personal and social development of young people. We create spaces in society where long term reflection and explicit development can complement the general rule of law. Youth work provides a setting outside the home for young people to develop interactions that claim their own dignity and give others equal respect. The informal nature of youth work allows personal choice beyond school structures where pupils can miss the underpinning quest for equality. In particular the character of youth workers themselves, the targets we set, and the explicit planned sessions we organise allow the learning for equality to have role models, a curriculum, and teaching materials.

Role models

Youth workers do not feature in many novels but the images of Rick Lemon in Adrian Mole's adolescence (Townsend, 1982), or Uncle Alan in *Anita and Me* (Syal, 1996) are both portrayals of emotionally sane, anti-racists in a world that is neither. Deliberate attempts by youth workers to try different ways of interacting between groups divided by race, religion, class, gender, nation, ability or sexuality are typical of youth work and they attract the support of adults who wish that they would succeed.

It is not always easy to set targets in this sort of work so what might youth workers do to explain their important work in building a more equal and inclusive society? The current outcomes associated with 'Make a positive contribution' (ECM, 2008) are often restricted to the most vulnerable young people. We could start to argue in detail at local level links that we can make between all young people's social development and the equality legislation. How, for example, are the young beneficiaries of affluence being equipped to moderate their abuse of social capital? Youth work's history in the settlement movement used to make opportunities for the public schools and Oxbridge students to make a positive contribution in the most deprived parts of Britain.

What targets could you set to increase equality across diverse populations?

Using insights from historic practice

Designing learning for equality should be a core activity of youth workers. Imaginative, affective, effective, long term, reflective, visible, coherent, accurate, informed learning programmes can respond to the twilight zone of racism at a local level and build the citizenship characteristics of an equal society. Vipin Chauhan's excellent report *Beyond Steel Bands and Samosas* (1989, p40) made recommendations to make a difference to young people's personal and social development.

RESEARCH SUMMARY

Chauhan's suggestions for practice

Enable learning:

- *history of how we formed unequal relationships in our society;*
- *learn about migrations of different people;*
- *understand civil and human rights;*
- *use diverse social, cultural, and recreational provision.*

Provide support:

- *to make relationships;*
- *in decision making and problem solving.*

Develop skills:

- *particularly for the more vulnerable groups;*
- *ensure support to gain key skills.*

Validate experiences:

- *include defining experiences in conversation and practice;*
- *Chauhan cites: schooling, growing up, being black in Britain, racism, migration, isolation, family, being 'back home'.*

Create environment:

- *display positive images;*
- *warm and comfortable place to go;*
- *specific meeting places: black only, women only, etc;*
- *provide the right environment, food, music, and a welcome.*

ACTIVITY **3.8**

- *Suggest a sequence of practical activities that might contribute in different ways to the practice of equality by young people based on race over a period of a year.*
- *Undertake the same task in relation to gender.*
- *Undertake the same task in relation to difference of sexuality.*

Key arguments when you are doing equality work

Here are some reasons why equality is a good thing, and why youth workers must try to achieve it.

- Equality is central to the way we live with each other in our society.

- Exclusion on any basis is contrary to a service for all young people.

- Equality is often challenged by people who abuse power. It suits them to maintain their advantage. We need to analyse who benefits from a challenge to inequality.

- Equality is associated with a vibrant society where all talents and interests are creative. A society that can include more people more effectively will flourish. It seeks to make the most of everyone's life.

- Inequality reflects a dehumanising and unfair use of resources that is associated with an arbitrary argument that destabilises the position of a group to advantage others. We need to analyse and rebut all arguments about the inferiority of sub-groups in society.

- Equality thrives when we get to know people who are not like us. When this is clear, and self evident we have learnt that difference is less important than achieving equality for all.

- Equality is an underpinning categorical imperative. Whatever we wish as the moral good, must be what we wish for all.

ACTIVITY 3.9

Review activity

The youth project you manage hosts a lesbian and gay support group for young people. There is no other setting in the town where lesbians and gays meet regularly; most go to a neighbouring city's gay village for their nights out. The support group is understandably discreet and facilitated by two volunteer youth workers.

The project has also developed a support project for African refugees who are based in the town. For them, this is a safe space away from the cramped accommodation where their families live.

Young people from this second group are with their parents after worship one week when they are asked about your project. 'Some people are gay, get over it' doesn't seem to be the right phrase for the young people to use as the conversation escalates with complaints that they are mixing with people who actively promote homosexuality. Parents are confused, young people are wounded and wonder what to do.

You get a text message and meet up with some of the young people. It is clear that they are unhappy and in danger of not being allowed to continue with the group.

• *Who do you seek to meet?*

• *What do you wish to discuss with them?*

• *Are there points that you will not concede?*

• *What points will you defend, and how?*

• *How does the concern for equality link to the values of association and listening?*

CHAPTER REVIEW

Social equality is both the equality of individual rights, and the fair treatment of others. The political and legal debates reflect the contested nature of the subject. The subsequent laws show the widespread acceptance of the benefits that come from giving and supporting equal rights. Youth work is a place for young people to develop an experience of being equal and recognising other people's equality. Youth workers need to intervene to develop groups and activities that improve the practice of equality.

FURTHER READING

Gore, Harriet (2007) Leading and managing anti-oppressive youth work, in Harrison, R, Benjamin, C, Curran, S and Hunter, R (eds) *Leading work with young people*. London: Sage. This article includes thoughtful reflection on youth work practice in the 1980s and 1990s.

Rattansi, Ali (2007) *Racism: a very short introduction*. Oxford: Oxford University Press. This slim book is a thorough and concise study.

Rawls, J (1971) *A theory of justice*, Cambridge, MA: Belknap Press of Harvard University. Rawls' argument develops the philosophy of human rights. It is a substantial and significant development of arguments about equality. The well-labelled sections and index help you explore particular points.

REFERENCES

Albemarle Report (1960) *The youth service in England and Wales*. London: HMSO.

Bion, W.R (1991) *Experiences in groups*. London: Routledge.

Blackadder (BBC series 3) *Dish and dishonesty.* Script by Curtis, R and Elton, B.

Boehmer, E (2004) Baden-Powell R (1908) *Scouting for boys*. Oxford: Oxford University Press.

Chauhan, V (1989) *Beyond steel bands and samosas*. Leicester: National Youth Bureau.

Commager, H S (1982) *The great declaration*. New York: Eastern National Park.

Devlin, P (1965) *The enforcement of morals*. Oxford: Oxford University Press.

ECM (2008) *Every child matters*. London: Department for Children Families and Schools.

Hart, H.L.A (1963) *Law liberty and morality*. Oxford: Oxford University Press.

Hunt Report (1967) *Immigrants and the youth service*. London: HMSO.

Jeal, T (1989) *Baden Powell*. London: Hutchinson.

Kant, I (1997) *Groundwork of the metaphysics of morals*. Cambridge: Cambridge University Press.

Lincoln, A (1907) *The speeches and letters of Abraham Lincoln*. London: Everyman.

Macpherson, W (1999) *The Stephen Lawrence inquiry 1999*. London: HMSO.

Niemoller, M (1959) Spoken in lectures at Union Seminary New York, reproduced in various ways including a musical version by the Kitchens of Distinction on the 'Disagreement of the People' COOKCD078 (CD, UK, June 1995).

Pecheul, A (2001) *Les dates clefs de la protection des droits de l'homme en France.* Paris: Ellipses.

Piaget, J (1977) *The Moral development of the child*. London: Penguin.

Rawls, J (1971) *A theory of justice*. Cambridge, MA: Belknap Press of Harvard University.

Roberts, J (1991) Two girls for every boy. *Youth and Policy,* 35: 8–13.

Robertson, G (2007) *The Levellers: the Putney debates.* London: Verso.

Rosenthal, M (1986) *The character factory*. New York: Pantheon.

Shorter Oxford English dictionary (1975) Oxford: Oxford University Press.

Syal, M (1996) *Anita and me*. London: Flamingo.

Tasker, D (1960) *Training the youth group*. London: Mowbray.

Thompson Report (1982) *Experience and participation*. London: HMSO.

Time Out (2006) *Berlin*. London: Ebury.

Townsend, S (1982) *The secret diary of Adrian Mole aged 13¾*. London: Puffin,

Williamson, H (2004) *The Milltown Boys revisited*. Oxford: Berg,

Chapter 4
Values: participation

C H A P T E R   O B J E C T I V E S

In this chapter I will explore the value of participation. Taking part is central to youth work. The voices and activities of young people indicate the energy level of participation. Participation is not only the here and now: it forms the life chances of the young person and society. Youth work *is concerned with facilitating and empowering the voice of young people, encouraging and enabling them to influence the environment in which they live.*

(National Occupational Standards, 2008, value 10)

The ubiquitous nature of participation can mean that we risk talking about it in a vague way. Think about the National Occupational Standards (NOS). The main area for participation is obviously working with others (3). However, young people need to participate by determining their own development (1), taking part in groups where there are equal rights and fairness (2) – see Chapter 3; deciding what the youth work will look like (4); and how the staff are managed (5). Participation principles need linking to effective co-operative practice with young people and the importance we have given to association, listening and equality.

Links to National and Professional Occupational Standards for Youth Work

Values	Principle activity area	Examples of Units
Participation:	3. work with others	1.1.3, 1.2.1, 1.2.2, 1.2.3, 1.2.4, 1.3.2, 1.3.3, 2.2.2, 3.1.2, 4.2.1, 4.2.5, 4.2.6, 4.4.1, 5.1.1, 5.1.2

Introduction

Transitions and participation

What do we expect of young people as they take part in society? Society uses several expectations of young people at the same time. This use of different, and sometimes contradictory, presuppositions reflects the transitional nature of youth work. The target age groups of youth work show the changing character of society and the active place it expects of young people.

Evaluate the contrast in 50 years of youth work.

- The youth service created by the Albemarle Report (1960) worked with 14–25 year olds. Young people left school at 14. They had their first job. However, they were not yet in their own home, or able to vote until they were 18. By 25 they might be 'settled' with their own house and family.

- Now (2009) work with young people focuses on 13–19 year olds. There are target groups for the more vulnerable from 11, and up to 25. Young people progress from compulsory school (13–17) to independent study or training, or work.

When youth workers consider young people's participation, which transition defines the intervention? Good youth workers need to identify the emphasis for a particular setting. Grotius (1646) expressed the changing character of a child's competence in law.

- A child has imperfect judgement. All of their acts are under the control of a parent.

- Judgement has matured and a child's actions are not subject to the parent's rule, although since the child remains at home parental control is proper if some family matter is at stake.

- The child is fully mature, complete in judgement and withdrawn from their family.

We will use the Grotius model, but will distinguish between what families and voluntary networks develop, and what the state establishes for young people. Here are our four definitions of young people's participation in society.

1 Young people are vulnerable children needing the care of adult professionals.

2 Young people are apprentice adults, gaining experiences to launch them into full adult participation in society.

3 Young people are public service users.

4 Young people are independent people in their own right with their own freedom, views and contribution in society.

Young people are vulnerable children needing the care of adult workers

The first definition emphasises that young people are not competent to take a full part in society. Decisions made by those under 18 lack maturity of thought and judgement. Adults make extra efforts for the young people who are vulnerable. We will look at both aspects.

Not giving children adult responsibility

Participation is limited. Society does not trust immature people with important decisions that have wider effects. Young people are not able to be charity trustees under 18, and they can't vote. They cannot legally participate in any equal sense under 18 on management committees as trustees. They cannot really engage in local council politics.

The argument is that children's judgement is unformed, insufficient to take on adult responsibility of complex judgements. John Locke's Treatise of Government said *Children are not born in this full state of equality, though they are born to it* (6: p55). There are some aspects of public life where children need to wait until they are old enough. In Scandinavia, they look at British imprisonment of children in disbelief: young people are not competent to break the law, just as they are not competent to exercise powers enshrined in law.

Adults having a duty to care for children

Complementing the lack of social status are the special efforts made by competent adults. Kant contrasted the freedoms of the parent and the child.

> *The act of procreation [is] one by which we have brought a person into the world without his consent and on our own initiative, for which deed the parents incur an obligation to make the child content with his condition so far as they can.*
>
> (Kant, 1996, p64)

Youth work can use Kant's argument as an assessment framework for young people. How do the parents of this young person make their child content with his condition? We can divide this question more precisely.

- How does each parent provide practical support?
- What regular engagement and conversations take place between child and parent?
- How does the parent nurture the increasing freedom of the child?

What happens when we make the judgement 'the parent seems incapable of putting the needs of their child before their own needs'? If she is in her early years, is it more likely that she would gain the support of the state to have the duty of care met than if she was a teenager? We can and do extend parental duty beyond the biological family to include the society in which the child grows up. The UN Convention on Rights of the Child does this: under 18 year olds are vulnerable, in need of special protection under the law, and the special help of professionals. Article 1 defines a child: *a child means every human being below the age of eighteen years*. For youth workers, this will mean that we work with children and adults. It is a useful reminder to all youth workers that you are the adult in the situation and should behave and think like one.

Basing the duty of care in Kant's argument has the benefit that he regards the child with the same respect as the adult. The child deserves the same consideration and needs help to find contentment in their situation. They are not a 'case'.

CASE STUDY

In the Cleveland Child Abuse Inquiry (1987), 59 of the abused were over 12. Lord Justice Butler-Sloss made these recommendations to professionals who communicate with children:

> *. . .The child is a person and not an object of concern.*

We recommend that:

a professionals recognise the need for adults to explain to children what is going on . . . and given some idea of what is going to happen to them;

CASE STUDY *continued*

b professionals should not make promises which cannot be kept to a child, and in the light of possible court proceedings should not promise a child that what is said in confidence can be kept in confidence;

c professionals should always listen carefully to what the child has to say and take seriously what is said;

d throughout the proceedings the views and the wishes of the child, particularly as to what should happen to him/her, should be taken into consideration by the professionals involved with their problems;

e the views and wishes of the child should be placed before whichever court deals with the case: we do not however, suggest that those wishes should predominate;

f those involved . . . should make a conscious effort to ensure that they act throughout in the best interests of the child (Butler-Sloss, 1987, p245).

ACTIVITY **4.1**

• How do activities in your youth work change when young people reach 18?

• Why is that justified?

• What specific activities do you restrict because the young people are under 18?

• Are there problems with this?

• Why are the restrictions justified?

• How do you communicate with the 'children' you work with?

Young people are apprentice adults, gaining experiences to launch them into full adult participation in society

The second definition emphasises ways in which young people are given space and support to try out adult responsibility. Young people show this apprenticeship in a variety of ways. One might be by a defined apprentice role, which may be unique to a young person. Another might be to imitate the adult practice; the risk here is that there is no significant difference between adult and young person's practice, leaving the young person vulnerable. In each case, the ethical issue is the extent to which adults create expectations about the outcomes of the young person's life.

Adults inducting young people into adult life

Article 29 of the UN charter seeks the education and preparation of young people as active citizens who share an understanding of an inclusive society of equal rights. How might we achieve this? Some organisations invite young people to take part in shadowing roles or as researchers so that they develop an understanding of the skills needed to take on the adult role when they are old enough. For example the Church of England organises a youth shadow event for the General Synod and this can prepare young people for the debates and procedures of that body. Again, political parties have intern and research roles for young people that enable them to take part with greater confidence and skill. Inter-generational opportunities like these provide young people with social capital and resilience. Rehearsing and skill development can be useful for young people who choose to take part and consent to prepare.

Youth work as a site of intergenerational activity

Some youth organisations, like the Boys' Brigade (BB), chose to imitate particular adult activities as the hallmark of their practice. The early days of the BB involved not just marching drills and bands but *Manual exercises for the rifle and carbine. . . and Firing Exercises* (MacFarlan, 1983, p37). Smith took that training from the militia to give adult discipline to unruly Sunday School lads (it also took away the need for the six weeks basic training when the Great War broke out). It is interesting that Baden-Powell attended a couple of big events for the BB (Jeal, 1989, p360ff) after the Boer War and spoke to the boys as the great military hero (who had survived a 200 day siege, and been promoted to General), and chose not to add these military trappings to his youth project.

The strength of both BB and Scouts has been in the growing responsibility and inter-generational work of regular membership. The risks lie in the possibility of the manipulation of the young person, or over interference by the adult. The Scouts use a 'participation wedge' (see Figure 4.1) to show leaders how much they need not to interfere. The logic is powerful: if

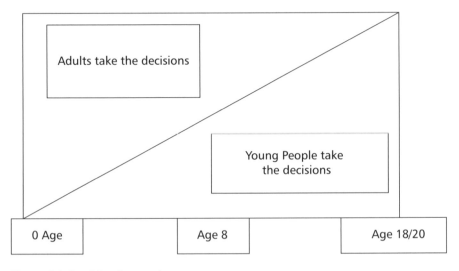

Figure 4.1 Participation wedge

these young people are moving from being dependent babes in arms, to 18 year olds who can vote and fight wars then they need to practice organising things themselves.

Who benefits from intergenerational activity?

The interaction between generations is of particular interest for voluntary groups who have reflected on the problems and opportunities in their training materials. A classic statement of this was written by the doyen of youth work educators, Fred Milson.

RESEARCH SUMMARY

Fred Milson (1981): 'four archetypes'

Milson identifies and explores contrasting stories from the Bible. Each story gives an insight into the role of young people within the community.

Abraham and Isaac (Genesis, 22: 1–9): youth sacrificed for an ideology.

Will Abraham sacrifice his only son? He is willing; at the last minute God saves the boy. The boy has no rights of his own except as a member of a family. 'Within all human associations older people will be tempted to sacrifice young people for their ideology; they are not merely socialised, but propagandised and indoctrinated. . . recruits for the cause.'

David and Abishag (1 Kings, 1: 1–3)

The elders of Israel run a beauty contest to find the young woman to warm the dying king's bed. He will surely arise, and lead them. 'The same thing happens today, almost literally, and certainly distastefully and offensively.'

Eli and Samuel (1 Samuel, 3: 1–10)

Samuel is acolyte to the priest Eli. The boy hears a voice call to him. He goes to Eli three times in the night, each time Eli denies that he called. Finally the old man understands what is happening. 'Eli does not explain. He points the boy forward, to find his own interpretation. . . Effective youth workers know when to be passive and when to be active.'

David and Solomon (1 Kings, 8: 12–21)

David, successful in so many things, came to his death bed having never built the temple he had wished. His disappointment and frustration is succeeded by Solomon's thorough building project. 'The young and old are not segregated, they have their conflicts, they also share moral and educational goals, which are mutually chosen.'

ACTIVITY 4.2

- *What examples can you give to match each of Milson's four archetypes?*

Relating the apprenticeship aspect of intergenerational work to Rawls' equality argument

Rawls (see Chapter 3) gives us a series of principles and rules to judge the fairness of social arrangements. Let us apply them to these approaches to youth work.

- Are there equal rights to an extensive system of equal liberties for all?

- Do the inequalities give the greatest benefit to the least advantaged?

- Is a less than equal liberty acceptable to those with lesser liberty?

- Are the social goods of youth work distributed equally, unless that unequal distribution is to the advantage of the least favoured?

The answer to all these questions is probably 'not yet.' There are forces moving the equality of participation in the right direction.

- Professional youth workers behaving fairly towards young people and using the values of youth work for all young people.

- Youth work organisations designed so that all can take part.

- Initiatives, like the old settlement movement, that seek out the most deprived as the beneficiaries of their resources.

- High levels of take up and respect accorded to voluntary organisations' youth work.

But

- Despite excellent redistributive work by national organisations, the material capacity of community and voluntary groups in rich areas is much greater than in other areas. Just contrast Guide groups: one has a small bag of equipment and meets in a school, the other has a purpose built hut. The closure of many youth clubs in the 1980s particularly hit the most disadvantaged areas (Layard and Dunn, 2009, p40).

- There are waiting lists for Scout groups, especially in the areas where it is hard to get suitable volunteers. (This is a little like the problem of GPs not working in these areas and perhaps a similar system of stipends might help.)

- Depending on the capacity of friends and relatives to help you become an adult can reproduce inequality in the next generation. Two thirds of the young people found their jobs in Kelby that way (MacDonald, 2005, p109): low paid and vulnerable like the others in the area. A study in other social groups might see the same process but with different results.

- Targeted work that tries to alter the equality balance is not always valued.

- Eighty per cent of young people complain they have nowhere to go (Layard and Dunn, 2009, p40).

Young people are service users

The third definition emphasises the expectation of public services that their users will give feedback on the service they receive. I will return to the issue of young people as service users of the youth service specifically in Chapters 6 and 7. Here I want to consider the wider issue of young people who engage with the state as service users; beneficiaries of services set up by the state for its citizens. I will address three questions.

- How does the state manage its power in contrast to the young person's vulnerability?

- How does the state best appoint advocates for young people, and professionals to empower young people within its own services?

- What is the nature and extent of competence recognised by the state when dealing with young people who are not yet adults?

How does the state manage its power in contrast to the young person's vulnerability?

First, we will look at the young person as vulnerable when faced with the power of the state's services. Parts of the UN Convention see the young person as a service user and place specific restrictions on the ways in which states may behave. They recognise the vulnerability of the young person in state provision, as the child previously discussed. Consider the contrast between a single young person and an established service. Services provided by professionals will be powerful in comparison with that young person. Each of the following characteristics separates the worker and the young person; together they exercise a powerful hegemony. Services are staffed by educated professionals, who work in teams, in developed roles, backed by robust systems of bureaucracy. These systems may even expect young people to contribute to achieve 360 degree feedback for the management of the service by adults. The young person new to the system is less articulate than the adults, and more interested in living his life than in being a service user. The buildings are strange and the paperwork is immense, if not incomprehensible. The UN list makes explicit principles to apply in services to manage this power conflict and address settings where there have been abuses of power.

Here are some of the UN Articles that apply to services for young people. First, there are general principles.

- Article 3: the best interests of the child shall be a primary consideration. (This is to be supported by legal intervention and sufficiently competent staff.)

- Article 6: the child has the inherent right to life.

- Article 8: the identity of a child is to be ensured.

- Article 16: a child is to be protected against arbitrary or unlawful interference with their privacy, family, home or correspondence.

Next there are Articles that refer to particular services of the state.

- Article 18: there should be institutions, facilities and services for the care of children. (This could include youth centres.)

- Article 19: the state shall act so that children are protected from abuse by all who care for them. (Expressed in Criminal Records checking, and intervening in the case of abuse.)

- Article 20: fostering and adoption services should be provided for children separated from parents. These services (Article 21) should be carefully controlled.

The state should protect vulnerable children:

- who are refugees (Article 22);

- who are disabled (Article 23);

- who need health care (Article 24);

- by providing periodic review of long term service dependents (Article 25);

- in need of social security (Article 26);

- in need of financial support from an absent parent (Article 27);

- by providing education (Article 28);

- to use their language (Article 30);

- to have access to culture and leisure opportunities (Article 31);

- not to be recruited to the armed forces (Article 38 and Optional Protocol 1);

- not to subject them to torture (Article 39);

- to treat them well within the legal system (Article 40).

ACTIVITY 4.3

- *Identify the current state services that address these Articles.*

- *What controls would you expect from these Articles on the state's use of physical force?*

- *What controls would you expect from these Articles on the state's use of information?*

The risk for young people is that the management of services designed to satisfy internal quality concerns of the organisation will take priority over the rights and needs of the child. When we address young people as service users and beneficiaries of organisations the core focus must be on the young person. The power of the organisation and professionals must be used to improve young people's lives. The core principles are that young people are vulnerable, that it is appropriate for services to advocate their best interests, and the challenge to services is to provide sufficient resources to make a difference.

How does the state best appoint advocates for young people, and professionals to empower young people within its own services?

Secondly, the state can use its power to protect, enable and empower young people. The Convention gives to children and young people rights explicitly associated with adults. Given what we have said earlier there needs to be empowerment of young people to achieve this autonomy of persons. The UN Convention sets a high standard and many countries are still trying to achieve this level. Recent UK legislation has increased the support given by the state to the advocacy and empowerment of young people.

Here are five links between Children Act 2004 and UN Convention.

1 The Children's Commissioner to ensure children's voice (2004 Act, Sections 5, 6 and 7), to make UN Article 12 a reality in the public sphere.

2 Local Safeguarding Children Boards as a statutory duty (2004 Act, Sections 10, 11, 13–16) to address for example UN Articles 6, 9, and 19.

3 A duty for local authorities to promote the educational achievement of looked after children and an associated power to transmit data relating to individual children in monitoring this (2004 Act, section 52 and 54) this corresponds with UN Articles 25 and 28.

4 Local Directors of Children's Services and a lead politician for this work (2004 Act, Sections 18 and 19) to ensure that the rights of Children are made a reality (UN Article 4).

5 Joint working between agencies is at the heart of the Act (2004 Act, Section 10). The Act explicitly empowers: the sharing of data (2004 Act, Section 12), Joint Area Reviews (2004 Act, Sections 20–24), pooled budgets, and the Children and Young People's plans (2004 Act, Sections 17); so that all levels of services for children and young people can help achieve the rights of all children (UN Article 4 again).

ACTIVITY **4.4**

- *Identify these roles in your local area.*

- *Explain how these jobs and processes advocate the best interests of young people.*

- *Describe how young people are empowered.*

What is the nature and extent of competence recognised by the state when dealing with young people who are not yet adults?

Thirdly, we will consider the competence of young people to make decisions to use the state power to affect their lives. It is important for young people to be involved in the decisions that affect their lives and this is part of current practice and legislation. UN Article 12 seeks the opportunity for a child to be heard *in any judicial and administrative proceeding affecting the child.* So, small children with a parent appear in courts, or are interviewed by workers discussing their care by a new adult in their lives. But as young people get older and more independent they wish to make their own decisions on their own. We will look at the way young people come to make decisions in the next chapter; here I want to discuss the state's engagement with young people as competent decision makers. The discussion is particularly important in the medical field.

Medical ethics: autonomy

Medical treatment is based on the principle of autonomy. You show autonomy by deciding what may or may not be done to you. A doctor gives you advice and it is up to you to take it. If a doctor treated you without consent it may be described as 'assault' or 'battery' (both are illegal). This would be because you had not agreed to the doctor touching or otherwise investigating, or treating, you.

Medical ethics: consent

We can define consent in more detail. Valid consent needs two things: the patient understands what is proposed, and the patient gives consent freely. The second part of this is fairly easy to determine by watching two people: the patient and another person. Does their interaction look like force, manipulation, intimidation or another abuse of power which would remove some element of the freedom that the patient ought to have to make a good decision?

The first element of consent, 'the patient understands what is proposed', is more difficult as it is happening inside the patient's own mind. We can use two tests to decide if the patient understands: capacity and competence. Capacity to decide generally requires the person to be of legal age and of sound mind. Legal ages are set for different activities: for sexual intercourse the legal age would be over 16. These ages are set to protect the vulnerable in social and emotional terms, and, perhaps, the physically immature. Sound mind means that it must be clear that they can make treatment decisions on their own behalf. The second test for competence to decide requires intelligence and understanding. Medical decisions are complicated and potentially life changing. The doctor needs to be sure that the person making the decision can comprehend and retain the treatment information. But for real understanding the patient needs to go beyond identifying the treatment elements. There needs to some sort of evaluation and judgement made by the patient. What are the risks? What choices are there? What are the benefits? Competence is seen when the patient weighs the information the doctor provides to arrive at a choice.

Applying competence to teenage conceptions

Teenage conception rates are a vexed ethical area for youth worker. We start with rules that set a clear boundary. The age of sexual consent at 16 is designed as a protection for the vulnerable: it is wrong for old men to have sex with under 18s. The law that protects all 18 year olds from adults reinforces this response to risk. Youth workers know that, after these rules, the decisions about what is good are more complicated. Youth workers do not have the training, powers and professional status of doctors, and yet they are often the adults with the opportunity to give young people good advice. Young people having sex are generally fit and well and so the management of their fertility does not sit so easily in the wider statements of how doctors deal with people who are sick and ill. From the advent of improved contraceptive techniques in the 1880s (Leathard, 1980, p6), to the establishment of state provided birth control in 1974 (Leathard, 1980, p228) the main source of advice had been, like youth work, in the voluntary sector. So, for reasons of opportunity, attitude to the young person and common approach in developing a more effective service youth workers are caught up in this area of the relationship of the state to young people. Youth workers can help young people understand the subtle choices they might make and increase the likelihood of the young person making a competent decision.

Teenage conceptions: an affair of the state

No matter how vexed the issue there is also the issue of scale and urgency. The scale of teenage conceptions in the UK makes young people's competence a matter for public concern and state engagement.

> The United Kingdom has the highest rate of teenage births in Western Europe.
> In 1998, the latest year for which comparable data is available, the UK rate was double that of Germany, three times that of France and five times the birth rate of the Netherlands.

> (Brook, 2008)

Its focus in particular neighbourhoods reflects a class divide that was evident in 1910–19 (when 60 per cent of class I used contraception compared with 39 per cent for class II and 33 per cent for class III) and in 1974 (Leathard, 1980, p7 and p171).

The reality is that young people under the legal age of consent have sex and fall pregnant. The evidence is that while some of the Neighbourhood Renewal Areas were successful in reducing rates on teenage conceptions, others were not (Blackman, 2006, p116). The clustering of teenage conceptions with other social exclusion factors (Blackman, 2006, p124) encourages the state to wish to intervene. We are talking about significant intervention, beyond a pleasant chat: in 1998 there was a 42.4 per cent rate of legal abortions among 15–17 year olds who were pregnant, by 2006 this was 48.9 per cent (Office for National Statistics and Teenage Pregnancy Unit, 2008).

ACTIVITY 4.5

Teenage pregnancy and social deprivation

Look at these contrasting figures and develop an argument about the differing levels of competence that they suggest.

Top ten English local authorities in 2006, source ONS	Rate of teenage pregnancies per 1000 under 18 year olds	Lowest ten local authorities in 2006, source ONS	Rate of teenage pregnancies per 1000 under 18 year olds
Lambeth	78.4	North Yorkshire	25.1
Southwark	75.0	Bath and North East Somerset UA	23.6
Nottingham UA	73.8	West Berkshire UA	23.6
Kingston upon Hull, City of UA	69.8	Dorset	22.7
Lewisham	68.2	North Somerset UA	22.6
Manchester	67.0	Kingston upon Thames	22.4
Blackpool UA	66.4	Buckinghamshire	21.3
Stoke-on-Trent UA	66.0	Windsor and Maidenhead UA	20.2
North East Lincolnshire UA	64.5	Wokingham UA	18.8
Hartlepool UA	64.5	Rutland UA	13.8
Scottish top three Local authorities in 2007, source ISD Scotland		**Scottish lowest three Local authorities in 2007 source, ISD Scotland**	
Dundee City	71.1	East Renfrewshire	21.1
Glasgow City	54.1	Argyll and Bute	20.4
North Ayrshire	48.9	Shetland Islands	16.1

ACTIVITY 4.5 *continued*

Wales top three local authorities In 2006, source ONS		Wales lowest three local authorities in 2006, source ONS	
Wrexham	58.9	Flintshire	34.2
Merthyr Tydfil	56.8	Carmarthenshire	33.5
Torfaen	56.1	Powys	31.8
N Ireland top five local authorities in 2005, source FPA in Northern Ireland and the Health Promotion Agency for Northern Ireland	% of all live births to under 20 year old mothers. NB Not the same scale see Note	N Ireland lowest five local authorities in 2005, source FPA in Northern Ireland and the Health Promotion Agency for Northern Ireland	% of all live births to under 20 year old mothers. NB Not the same scale see Note
W Belfast	14.4	Strabane	3.7
N Belfast	12.5	Dungannon	3.7
Derry	8.4	Magherafelt	3.6
Coleraine	8.3	Armagh	3.4
E Belfast	8.3	Omagh	3.2
Source: General Register Office/ Project Support Analysis Branch	**Births per 1000 females 13–19**		**Births per 1000 females 13–19**
Deprived areas	28.9	Non-Deprived areas	12.4
Northern Ireland	16.1		

Source: Health and Social Care monitoring Bulletin 2: 2007
Note: Northern Irish statistics are hard to obtain in a comparable form. The 2000 report on teenage pregnancy for the Department of Health, Social Services and Public Safety gives an overall rate among 18-year-old women in 1998 of 50 per 1000.

When we try to work out what is good in this area we need to bring the facts of young people's lives closer to the ethical codes that determine practice. We need to define consent so that young people, who act independently as sexual agents in fact, can have that independence recognised in law. This can benefit the young person by increasing their autonomy and allowing them to manage the risks they face for themselves. Good contraceptive advice, education and provision can help young women reduce the risks of unwanted pregnancy; and it is best set in a programme that addresses their whole lives (Blackman, 2006, p125) – ideal for youth work. It also prevents our laws and ethics looking foolish.

Parental consent

The debate focuses on a parent consenting to treatment on behalf of their child. Given the earlier rules about competence being linked to age, it will be no surprise that historically the parent was given the responsibility to decide about what would happen to the child. If those are the responsibilities of being a parent, the other question is: can young people get independent advice without their parents' knowledge? Two case studies highlight the dilemmas and changing practice.

> CASE STUDY
>
> ### Telling the parents
>
> *In 1971 Dr Browne, a Birmingham GP, told the parents of a 16 year old that she was on the pill. He did this without the patient's consent. (Leathard, 1980, p145)*

What effect would the story above have on young people?

> CASE STUDY
>
> ### Fraser guidelines: young people and contraception
>
> *Victoria Gillick brought a case to the House of Lords (1985). Mrs Gillick challenged her health authority's right to prescribe abortion and contraception for her under 16-year-old daughters without parental consent. In the judgement Lord Fraser made a statement about how to determine competence that applies to young people and contraception*
> *(British Medical Journal 11 April 2006).*
>
> *In 1985, the House of Lords held that a child under 16 was competent to consent to contraceptive treatment without parental knowledge or agreement. Lord Fraser set the following tests for professionals to use.*
>
> *1. Does the young person understand the potential risks and benefits of the treatment and advice given? (Competence.)*
>
> *2. Why does the young person not want their parents to provide their support in this decision?*
>
> *3. Is the young person is likely to begin or continue having sexual intercourse?*
>
> *4. Will the young person's physical and/or mental health suffer if they do not receive contraceptive advice or supplies or treatment?*
>
> *5. Is it in the young person's best interests to receive contraceptive advice and/or treatment without parental consent?*

What can youth workers do that is useful and good for young people, in the light of this guidance?

Review of the role of young people as service users

We are balancing three elements.

1 Young people participate in state services as vulnerable, less powerful actors.

2 Young people can benefit from professionals who are there to redress power imbalances.

3 Young people can be competent to make significant decisions about their well being.

Young people are independent people in their own right with their own freedom, views and contribution in society

The fourth definition emphasises the simple uniqueness of each person, no matter what age they are. In Chapters 2, 3 and 4 we have looked at four broad themes that define young people's place in society: association, listening, equality and participation. You could be left with the impression from the discussion about service delivery that young people are weak participants in the state and that this is a good thing to be ensured by youth workers. I wish to end the chapter with an argument that does not agree with this.

I compared the values we express with verbs: they are processes and changing states in people's lives. Applying values to young people's lives is ideal because it is clear that they are also changing: they are *in a period of their transitions from dependence to independence* (PAULO, 2002, piv). The professional youth worker is like the kayaker or surfer catching a wave: at their best they make it look effortless as they align surface and churning water. Our admiration is due in part to the knowledge that it isn't easy, and the forces are as unwieldy as adolescence. The verbs that youth work lives with should be ones that give young people greater freedom. Here we will look at three of those forces.

Growing up and getting older

The first major force is the inevitable one of aging. Young people move to adult responsibility simply by getting older. Playing this wave should mean working on the presupposition that becoming adults is the direction of flow. We should suspect as bad practice those choices and policies that restrict young people's freedom by looking backwards rather than forwards; treating them as children. This is why Lord Fraser's guidelines are wise. The direction of flow is that young people are more likely to have sex as they age. If we think there are risks (and it is generally health and safety that is cited to stop things happening) then we need to devise ways for young people to learn what they need to, and practise skills that will be helpful. We understand this in paddling rivers: start on flat water, and build up through more difficult white water before you surf the waves. What are the steps needed to help young people manage the risks for themselves?

You are not alone

The second force is the need to live with others. Young people leave the family they were born into to become part of a wider world. Association by young people is an inevitable occurrence and prepares people for love, work, political activity, creative performance, recreation, and so on. We should suspect as bad practice choices and policies that restrict young people's freedom by controlling who and why they can meet. If we think there are risks (and they are claimed to be to public order) then we need to devise ways for young people to learn what they need to, and practise skills that will be helpful. Overcrowded houses and lousy British weather mean that good youth work needs warm and safe places to meet.

I do not wish you to think that all association is a natural force. Popper usefully distinguishes between a closed society and an open society. The closed society makes no distinction between social life and nature (Popper, 2003, vol. 1, p184). It may reinforce this unchangeable social life by reference to magic, tribal distinctiveness, cultural characteristics or even storytelling using apparently scientific data. Popper uses Sparta's policies to illustrate resistance to opening a society. Popper was writing in response to Hitler, but it is not difficult to make links to popular local neighbourhood politics in the UK.

- Protect tribal habits and shut out foreign influence.

- Anti-humanitarianism: shut out equalitarianism, democratic and individualistic ideologies.

- Autarchy: be independent in trade.

- Anti-universalism: distinguish your tribe from others.

- Mastery: dominate and enslave your neighbours.

- Do not become too large: keep identity and unity.   (2003, vol. 1, p195)

The open society is one where individuals are confronted with personal choices and can take decisions (2003, vol. 1, p186). Popper quotes Athenian democrats to illustrate the characteristics of rational decision making undertaken in groups.

> *Democritus: Not out of fear but out of a feeling of what is right should we abstain from doing wrong. . .Virtue is based, most of all, upon respecting the other person.*
> (2003, vol. 1, p198)

> *Pericles' funeral oration: Our administration favours the many instead of the few: this is why it is called a democracy. . . We consider a man who takes no interest in the state not as harmless, but as useless; and although only a few may originate a policy, we are all able to judge it. We do not look upon discussion as a stumbling block but as an indispensible preliminary to acting wisely.*
> (2003, vol. 1, p199)

For young people just being there hoping to see history unfold will not do. Popper rightly contends that history has no meaning. The young people we encourage to take part grow in competence and their own social and personal capacities, such that they are able to give meanings to the events they make happen (2003, vol. 2, p307). Participation is about turning up, and being competent in groups that associate (Chapter 2), and seeking greater equality (Chapter 3), and developing your own moral sense (Chapter 5). How will we give them the skills to meet new people, cross cultural boundaries, and treat others equally no matter what they learnt at home? What are the steps needed to help young people manage association for themselves?

A progressive society seeking equality

The third force is the deep seated desire of our society to develop equality. I quote the UN Convention because it reflects a global commitment to challenge the imposition of inequality, often by violent means. Equality provokes arguments because (as I mentioned in Chapter 3) it does not suit simple majorities. But equality has been built up because the alternatives are so offensive: abuse of women, slavery for black people, and so on. We should suspect as bad practice choices and policies that restrict young people's freedom by making choices on the basis of who they are. Counting heads, assessing achievement are essential tools to make these judgments. If some elements of the young population of our area are not part of our youth work then we are not giving everyone an equal chance. We may have taken the chicken chute rather than paddling the whole river. As Rainborough argued: *for really I think that the poorest he that is in England has a life to live, as the greatest he.*

Review activity

We have looked at four different ways in which society expects young people to take part. Each requires matching and different responses from youth workers. What are the behaviours that will best match each approach to young people's place in society?

Young people	Youth work behaviours
Vulnerable children	
Apprentice adults	
Public service users	
Independent people in their own right	

CHAPTER REVIEW

Participation shows a young person's free membership of society. There are excellent highways to participation, built by people who fulfil Kant's duty to the vulnerable young. In each generation, our society develops inventive, creative, just, fair, passionate individuals who repay the investment. The challenge is to balance our care for young people with their grasp of their own freedom. Infantilising them for their vulnerability or bureaucratising their lives to fit our roles does not help them. In the old story, David freely rejected King Saul's adult armour and slew Goliath who had terrified his society (1 Samuel, 17: 38ff).

FURTHER READING

Badham, B and Davies, T, The active involvement of young people, in Harrison, R Benjamin, C, Curran, S and Hunter, R (eds) (2007) *Leading work with young people*. London: Sage.

Batsleer, J (2008) *Informal learning in youth work*. London: Sage.

Edmonds, D and Eidinow, J (2001) *Wittgenstein's poker*. London: Faber. This book has seen the downfall of German and Soviet totalitarianism, and provides good arguments to improve our own democracy.

MacDonald, R and Marsh, J (2005) Disconnected youth. Basingstoke: Palgrave Macmillan.

Popper, K (2003) *The open society and its enemies.* London: Routledge (2 volumes). This is highly readable and remains a powerful argument for free democracy. Popper recalled an incident before Hitler came to power in Germany when he met a young man from Carinthia in Nazi uniform and carrying a pistol: *He said to me, What, you want to argue? I don't argue. I shoot.*

REFERENCES

Albemarle Report (1960) *The youth service in England and Wales.* London: HMSO.

Blackman, T (2006) *Placing health.* Bristol: Policy Press.

Butler-Sloss, E (1987) *Report of the inquiry into child abuse in Cleveland 1987.* London: HMSO.

Grotius, H (1964 [1646]) *The law of war and peace [De jure belli et pacis],* tr. Francis W. Kelsey, 3 vols. New York: Oceana.

Jeal, T (1989) *Baden Powell.* London: Hutchinson.

Kant, I (1996) *The metaphysics of morals.* Cambridge: Cambridge University Press.

Layard, R and Dunn, J (2009) *A good childhood.* London: Penguin.

Leathard, A (1980) *The fight for family planning.* London: MacMillan.

MacFarlan, D.M (1983) *First for boys: the story of the Boys Brigade 1883–1983.* Glasgow: Collins.

Milson, F (1981) *Youth in the local church.* Leicester: NYB.

NOS (2008) National and professional occupational standards for youth work. London: LLUK.

PAULO (2002) *National occupational standards for youth work.* Grantham: PAULO.

Popper, K (2003) *The open society and its enemies.* London: Routledge.

Robertson, G (2007) *The Levellers: the Putney debates.* London: Verso.

WEBSITES

Brook (2008) **www.brook.org.uk/content/M6_4_teenage%20pregnancy.asp**

Children Act 2004 **www.opsi.gov.uk/Acts/acts2004/ukpga_20040031_en_1**

Office for National Statistics **www.statistics.gov.uk/hub/**

Teenage Pregnancy Unit 2008 **www.everychildmatters.gov.uk/teenagepregnancy/**

UN Convention of the Rights of the Child **www.unicef.org/crc/**

Chapter 5

Developing ethical reflection by young people

CHAPTER OBJECTIVES

This chapter is about young people as moral beings: people who develop ethically thoughtful actions. Young people, like all of us, make judgements about what is good and bad, and act in ways that are good and bad.

- The news is bloodied by a teenager dying from a knife used by another young person.

- The film *Juno* tells the story of a young woman who falls pregnant and chooses adoption rather than abortion.

- Young people are giving their time to others to make the world a better place.

- What example can you give of young people making moral choices?

Youth work and youth workers are part of this moral world. My focus in this chapter is the young people themselves, and my aim for youth workers is that they might facilitate ethical reflection by young people and the development of a beneficial adult pattern of moral behaviour.

Links to National and Professional Standards for Youth Work

Values	Principle activity area	Examples of Units
Young people's development	1. Facilitate the personal, social and educational development of young people	1.1.1, 1.1.3, 1.1.4, 1.2.1, 1.3.1
	2. Promote equality and young people's interests and welfare	2.2.2, 2.3.3

I will describe and analyse some theories of moral development, and particularly the ways in which these might be used with young people. I will give you a couple of examples of moral formation in youth work – one bad and one good. I will then explore areas of the lives of young people that worry adults and make them wish to see moral development in the lives of young people: learning and work, and sex. I will also consider areas where young people make ethical choices, and quite often consider that older people are ethically weak or immoral: global justice and animal rights. The final part of the chapter looks at the use of two big historical themes related to humanisation; bad behaviour between people that can be used to stimulate wider moral development of young people.

Moral development theory

The moral development of people, children in particular, has been the subject of considerable study. Jean Piaget and Lawrence Kohlberg used their studies to suggest stages that young people seem to go through naturally. These studies have been very influential in the whole field of education, formal and informal, and school organisation has changed as a result. Their work in cognitive developmental psychology also led to related studies in places where the moral development of people has been an explicit expectation. James Fowler and John Westerhoff have developed studies of the way in which moral and religious development happens among Christians who expect to learn and change in these areas of their lives. You can see from the way I have introduced this that there is a tension that we live with between the descriptive analysis of the psychologist who sees things as they are, and the intervention of the educator who is hopeful about the opportunities each person might take up.

Jean Piaget

Jean Piaget made a major impact on our understanding of how children and young people grow and change. Piaget's pioneering work in Switzerland between 1925 and 1980 was very productive: 50 books and 500 papers. You can get a taste for his ideas from the thought provoking, accessible book, published in 1932, which is widely available in English as *The Moral Judgement of the Child* (Piaget, 1977).

Piaget's study spots a change in moral reasoning at about 10–12 years old. What is the child's view about morality? Before they are ten, rules seem to come from adults, or God, and the child can't change them; all the child can do is consider the consequences. From 10–12 years children begin to be interested in the intentions of why people do things: what are their motives? Rules are seen by that older group as ways in which we get on together.

Piaget's significance for youth workers

How might Piaget be useful for youth workers? You might argue that the moral shift happens before a child reaches youth work. But being a morally autonomous person takes some getting used to. Youth workers use the insight from Piaget each time they negotiate ground rules in a group: affirming that these are young people who can create rules (they don't just do what we say in some God-like role). A group's ground rules allow young people to try out ways of putting into words 'ways in which we get on together'. Getting those words right is not easy and it is not a problem in youth work to do the task frequently. But for youth workers – especially the old hands – we know what makes a group get on and so it can be tempting to skip the ground rules. Piaget reminds us that the young people we work with may be doing this consciously for the first time in a world where their Mam still 'grounds me' and they must do what the behaviour code at school says.

Lawrence Kohlberg

Kohlberg developed Piaget's insights, making a model of moral development more complex, and building up a generation of work from the 1960s onwards. A good book bringing together much of his material is by Power, Higgins and Kohlberg (1989). Table 5.1 shows a brief outline of Kohlberg's model.

Table 5.1 Kohlberg's model of moral development

Stage	Characteristics	Typical concerns of the moral agent at this stage
Pre-conventional morality		
1	Obedience and punishment	I must obey or I will be punished
2	Individualism and exchange	Is it fair?
Conventional morality		
3	Good interpersonal relations	What motives lie behind the action?
4	Maintain social order	What are the legal limits for behaviour?
Post-conventional morality		
5	Social contract and individual rights	We need to take part in forming laws as an expression of our democratic lives.
6	Universal principles	There are categorical imperatives which we will express in our behaviour.

Kohlberg groups his six stages into three groups, and the first two groups reflect Piaget's model. His third pair move towards the philosophical concerns expressed about moral behaviour, stage 6 being particularly linked to moral beacons such as Kant or Gandhi. Kohlberg's initial study of 72 boys in Chicago was developed by reinterviewing them as they got older, and by doing other studies. By the end of his life in 1987 he had undertaken studies in over forty western and non-western countries, showing increasing subtlety in moral judgement with age and education and confirming the main stages in moral reasoning he had identified (Kuchinke, 2001, p191).

Kohlberg's significance for youth workers

Why is Kohlberg interesting? First: because he describes a world where people make moral judgements in quite different ways because of their personal and social development. Second: because the ideal behaviour hoped for by the moral philosophers is something that is very unusual in his sample, indeed few show behaviour typical of level 5. Third: because of the related research and debate. For example, Carol Gilligan (1982) has argued that the male sample in his early study may reflect a different developmental process to female subjects and that young men may express morality as justice while young women may do so in terms of care. Kohlberg welcomed the debate: *he believed that without cognitive conflict and dialogue, we cease to develop* (Kuchinke, 2001, p192).

Piaget, Kohlberg and the moral education of young people

Both Piaget and Kohlberg help us understand more about how people develop. We have embedded so many of their insights into our normal life that it can be difficult to believe that we thought any differently before. Piaget's life project was to try to combine the benefits of science, in making knowledge out of facts, and the benefits of religion, which is value laden (Smith, 2001, p38). Kohlberg said that the beginning of his work was rooted in the experience of Nazi tyranny while he was at school and college. His interest in morality and moral education: *arose in part as a response to the Holocaust and the slow but continuing effort of world society to make some sense of it.* (Kohlberg, 1981, in Kuchinke, 2001, p189). In both cases they were dealing with the contradiction between two areas of life that sit alongside each other in our experience: the growing body of evidence based knowledge and understanding; and the nature of expressing values and morals in human life.

Education and morality in Germany (1900–1945)

Learning as such does not necessarily produce ethical behaviour. Following von Humboldt's reforms in the nineteenth century German society educated more of its people to a higher standard than other nations in Europe. By 1914, at the outbreak of the First World War, illiteracy rates were 1 in 1000 in the German army, compared to 1 in 68 in the French, 1 in 220 in the Austro-Hungarian, and 1 in 330 in the Italian armies (Bosworth, 2005, p40). Illiterate soldiers were 15 times more common in the French army than their German opponents at Verdun. The *Einsatzgruppen* of the 1940s, who organised the massacres in the early stages of the holocaust: *were not criminals, sadists and maniacs, but were drawn from the elite of the German professional middle class. . . there were more PhD graduates among them than in any other unit of the German army. They were handpicked for their strong ideological motivation and reliability* (Bresheeth et al., 1994, p75). Of the 25 *Einsatzgruppen* and *Einsatzkommando* leaders, 15 of them bore the title of PhD, most of them doctors of jurisprudence or philosophy (ARC, 2006). This model of national educational success produced immoral behaviour of staggering proportions: the deaths of between 4.8 and 6.2 million Jews (Davies, 1996, p1328). Simply being educated may not lead to acceptable moral learning.

However, closer examination of the moral and social development of young people under the Nazis shows elements of moral formation. You will know about both the widespread use of propaganda and the attacks on Jewish scholars, as ways of vilifying the Germans who were Jews. Nietzsche provided a philosophical approach (see Chapter 8) to underpin the Nazi self-awareness as the master race. More specifically for youth workers is the experiential learning young people received in the *Hitlerjugend*. This became the dominant youth service. Perhaps you have a propaganda picture of blonde, fit young people walking the Bavarian Alps, like a scene from the Sound of Music, or the mass rally of young people in Leni Riefenstahl's film *The Triumph of the Will*. The German history museum in Berlin exhibits a large sheath knife typical of the *Hitlerjugend*. The label explains that about 600 young people died on summer camps. If this covered the short period of Hitler's peacetime government (1933–39) this is a high accident rate. If we place this alongside other aspects of Fascism, which increased the frequency and legitimacy of violence, we might read this knife in the *Hitlerjugend* as moral preparation for the wounding and killing of other people. Under Nazi rule, there were *acts of violence carried out quite openly* (Klee et al., 1991, p1). The *Hitlerjugend* was powerful in a social development of young people. They proved resolute, committed to the Nazi cause to very last struggle in Berlin: *a smaller size of steel helmet had been manufactured for boy soldiers, one of the last public photographs of Hitler shows him as he caresses one of his youngest defenders, watched by Artur Axmann, head of the Hitler Youth* (Beevor, 2002, p235 and plate 29).

Learning right and wrong from a curriculum that includes deliberately immoral content can show the power of what we learn as teenagers. Developing moral autonomy, responsibility and sound judgement as part of each person's education requires the sort of personal and social development typical of the best youth work. It is rooted in the balance of individual freedom and equality discussed in earlier chapters. Moral neutrality is also a moral position; the challenge is to develop effective moral education within youth work. You will have heard the response to a public statement of moral abdication: *That's what they said at Nuremberg* – referring to the trials of the Nazi leaders after the war.

Moral education in faith based youth work

Faith based youth work has been persistently optimistic about the creation of good moral behaviour in young people. The group will provide peer support for counter cultural values (YMCA), and the adult youth worker will give encouragement for the development of good behaviour (Maude Stanley). However, a crude transmission of the values from one generation to another is not going to work. Piaget reported that children stop simply believing what the adults have told them when they are over 12, they need to develop their own values. Kohlberg reported changing stages of moral behaviour during people's lives, and these need the space and stimulus for their development. Fowler and Westerhoff have each developed these themes as 'faith development' and there is now a considerable literature which faith based workers, particularly, will find worth pursuing.

ACTIVITY **5.1**

Fowler's life map

James Fowler has encouraged the use of 'Life Maps' for people to plot out how they thought and behaved in different ways at different times in their lives. It is a good exercise to encourage reflection by youth workers. Each person draws a time line for their life. They mark on it what was happening at different points up to the present. Then each person should go back over contrasting times and try to express at several points (Fowler often uses four points: childhood, adolescence, present, and a possible future).

- *What was important to you, giving your life meaning at the time?*

- *What was faith to you? (Fowler's question)*

- *(Or we might ask:) What was morally important for you?*

The reflection is more effective if it is done with sufficient time (two hours) to prepare and to discuss it with a couple of other people who you trust. An exercise like this is likely to make you reflect on the stages of development highlighted by the studies.

Living with personally diverse moral positions

Firstly: we don't simply move from one way of being moral to another, we may continue to experience other 'stages' even though we live mainly in a particular stage. As an adult I might be living mainly in Kohlberg stage 5: happy to be part of a democratic society where we make and apply complicated, agreed rules, taking part in managing a public service where those rules are formed and expressed, perhaps campaigning and lobbying to get bad rules changed. Nevertheless, I might have the experience of visiting my parents and find I am treated as I was when I was a small child (stage 1). Or I might discuss sharing my grandparent's things out fairly with the rest of the family (stage 2). Or, I might grasp a categorical imperative to reduce my carbon footprint and stop driving a car (stage 6). These last three examples may not be how I generally behave, but they do remind me of how I might be. It seems to me important that we affirm the value of these glimpses, especially given the weak evidence for stage 6 as a dominant phase, and the social need for stage 6 in challenging immoral behaviour. This practice of stage 6 morality by someone not generally 'at that stage' is vividly captured in the story of Oskar Schindler, and can be found in others, such as the joint action of the Danish people in saving so many of the Danish Jews.

The impact of our moral development on other people

Secondly: our viewpoint from a particular dominant stage affects the way we intervene in the lives of another's moral development. Let us look at the relation between the moral development of the youth worker and that of the young person. Youth workers don't develop morally just by getting older. A combination of active learning and reflection on life experience leads to moral change.

CASE STUDY

Let us use Kohlberg's stages to analyse three youth workers' impact on young people.

1 Gemma's moral perspective is at the Pre-conventional stages (1 and 2). She has the health and safety rules; and will follow them to the letter. She only uses the prepared risk assessments; and will not argue for work that steps outside these boundaries.

2 Martin is at the Conventional stages (3 and 4). When disputes happen in the group, he is good at thinking through the motives that lie behind what has happened. He is well aware of the legal limits for behaviour.

3 Bryony is at the Post-conventional stage (5 and 6). She is keen to get the group to express the rules from scratch. She is committed to campaigns and political action. She can write policy from the beginning.

Each of these workers can have an impact on the moral development of the young people they work with.

• Gemma will assert the rightness of a particular act. But she will not tease out reflection to achieve understanding either in the organisation or among young people. The lack of

---

discussion may keep the moral development of the young people at the level they started.

- *Martin will focus on the group and what it does. He will care about the interactions and what has been agreed to keep the work inside the law. This is useful in the transition from young people's peer group or family to a wider social setting. He will model a robust way of behaving in groups which will help young people develop personal responsibility. But he may seem a bit limited or old fashioned as they get older and suspect that there are nuances to some of these choices.*

- *Bryony will give the young people a sense of living in a wider world where they are being introduced to challenges beyond the youth work setting. She is curious about the decisions that they make and might be faced with. She wants to raise their game in their ability to decide, so she designs opportunities for moral decision making. She is interested in encouraging the curiosity the young people have to change the rules of the game so that they might be a bit fairer.*

Gemma, Martin and Bryony have their equivalents wherever youth work takes place.

Review of moral development theories

You may find this argument frustrating and wish to reply: How can I be good enough? Why would I want to be good like that? Surely moral educators are hypocrites and arrogant? I think that this separates the values too much from the facts; Piaget tried to bring them together to grasp more effectively what goes on in moral development. Youth work is a value based activity and so we are faced inevitably with questions about our reflection on those moral values. Fortunately, we have plenty of small practical ways of expressing those values in programmes, so we do not need to be too overwhelmed by grand moral judgements. In this next part I will suggest ways in which common developmental themes for young people are used as sites of moral development. The role of the youth worker is to design activities to enhance young people's decision making skills.

Learning in the context of national policy

If you liked school you'll love work writes Irving Welsh. There is a similar tradition in youth work of being sour about both. The positive impact of mainstream youth work on the life chances of the most deprived have been given a fairly hard time by the study of those born in 1970 and who were 16 in the depths of 1986 (Feinstein *et al.*, 2006). Youth club work, unlike uniformed organisations, church based work, and sporting activities, seems to have a link to poor long term outcomes as adults. While there is a debate about the nature of causation and correlation (see the various versions of the Feinstein research publication), it is fair to challenge youth workers to raise their game in encouraging young people to become effective lifelong learners. Current practice can be too casual about devising 'accredited outcomes' to little benefit for the young people. In this section we will look at what drives the National Curriculum used in secondary schools and how it fits with what youth workers do. I then want to draw out three themes to support the development of the young people as they manage their learning.

ACTIVITY 5.2

The National Curriculum's aim, purpose and values

Read this edited version of the 2008 National Curriculum for the education of teenagers in the secondary phase in England and Wales. Discuss the extent to which the aim and values match those of youth work.

Education influences and reflects the values of society.
Aim: for all young people to become:

- *successful learners;*

- *confident individuals living fulfilling lives;*

- *responsible citizens.*

Purpose of the curriculum to:

- *promote the spiritual, moral, cultural, mental and physical development of learners;*

- *prepare learners at school for adult life.*

A national curriculum:

- *is an entitlement, for all pupils, to learning and to develop knowledge, understanding, skills and attitudes necessary for their self-fulfilment and development as active and responsible citizens;*

- *sets standards for learning and attainment;*

- *promotes continuity and coherence, ensuring progression in learning, facilitating the transition of pupils between phases of education;*

- *promotes shared understanding of the work of schools and the learning resulting from compulsory education.*

In particular the curriculum should:

- *raise attainment, particularly in English, mathematics, science and ICT;*

- *ensure entitlement for all learners to a broad, balanced and relevant curriculum that offers continuity and coherence and secures high standard;*

- *induct learners into the subject disciplines and to develop specialisms appropriate to aptitude;*

- *prepare young people for the world of employment and further and higher education;*

ACTIVITY 5.2 *continued*

- *make learners more aware of, and engaged with, their local, national and international communities;*

- *encourage learners to take responsibility for their own health and safety, and appreciate the benefits and risks of the choices they make;*

- *contribute to community cohesion;*

- *acknowledge, promote and pass on the core knowledge and skills valued by society to the next generation.*

Values underpinning the curriculum:

- *education should reflect the enduring values that contribute to personal development and equality of opportunity for all, a healthy and just democracy, a productive economy, and sustainable development; these include values relating to:*

- *the self, recognising that we are unique human beings capable of spiritual, moral, intellectual and physical growth and development;*

- *relationships as fundamental to the development and fulfilment of ourselves and others, and to the good of the community: we value others for themselves, not only for what they have or what they can do for us;*

- *the diversity in our society, where truth, freedom, justice, human rights, the rule of law and collective effort are valued for the common good: we value families, including families of different kinds, as sources of love and support for all their members, and as the basis of a society in which people care for others; we also value the contributions made to our society by a diverse range of people, cultures and heritages;*

- *the environment, both natural and shaped by humanity, as the basis of life and a source of wonder and inspiration which needs to be protected;*

- *responding positively to the opportunities and challenges of the changing world in which we live and work: we take up roles of individuals, parents, workers and citizens meeting economic, social and cultural change, including globalisation of the economy and society, new work and leisure patterns and the rapid expansion of communications technologies.*

Lifelong learners

The development of lifelong learners fits with youth work's role as an educational activity and its commitment to 'growing real persons'. Good practice over the last 20 years has seen youth workers devising ways of getting young people back into learning, who have failed or been excluded. There were major debates about the rightness of changing from one unemployment support programme to the next. Most youth workers now argue for the benefits for young people to take control of their own lives and find ways of earning a living to support themselves and their dependents. In some places the commitment to learning was fired by Freire and Gramsci and built an enthusiasm for young people finding freedom

C H A P T E R   R E V I E W

Encouraging young people to develop their own ethical standpoint is part of ethical behaviour by youth workers. We can see from the research that moral development takes important steps forward in the teenage years. We know that the issues facing young people are contested and opportunities for the abuse of power. Finally the anxieties about the risks faced by young people mean that we hope they will make wise choices. Green and Christian (1998) captured the role of adults in the moral development of young people well in their choice of 'accompanying' as the key theme. Increasingly we walk alongside young people who are making their own minds up about what is good.

FURTHER READING

Benigni's film about the Holocaust in Italy *Life is beautiful.*

If you haven't watched Leni Riefenstahl's film *The Triumph of the Will* on YouTube some of the young people you work with will have.

Bresheeth, H, Hood, S and Jansz, L (1994) *The Holocaust for beginners*. Cambridge: Icon Books. A more accessible graphic book of the Holocaust.

Gilbert, M (1986) *The Holocaust: the Jewish tragedy.* London: Collins. A great study of the Holocaust.

Spiegelman, A (1986) *Maus.* London: Penguin.

Spielberg's *Schindler's List.* film about the Holocaust

Thomas, H (1999) *The slave trade: the story of the Atlantic slave trade 1440–1870* New York: Simon and Schuster.

Films can be a way into talking about slavery: *Amistad*, *Roots*, and *Amazing Grace.*

REFERENCES

Beevor, A (2002) *Berlin*. London: Penguin.

Bosworth, R.J.B (2005) *Mussolini's Italy.* London: Penguin.

Bresheeth, H, Hood, S and Jansz, L (1994) *The Holocaust for beginners*. Cambridge: Icon Books.

Bunt, S (1975) *Jewish youth work.* London: Bedford Square Press.

Davies, N (1996) *Europe.* Oxford: Oxford University Press.

Eager, W.M (1953) *Making men.* London: University of London Press.

Feinstein, L Bynner, J, Duckworth, K (2006) Young people's leisure contexts and their relation to adult outcomes. *Journal of Youth Studies*, 9(3): pp. 305–327.

Fowler J (1981) *Stages of faith.* San Francisco Harper and Row.

Freire, P (1985) *The politics of education.* Basingstoke: Macmillan.

Gilligan, C (1982) *In a different voice: psychological theory and women's development.* Cambridge: Harvard University Press.

Green, M and Christian, C (1998) *Accompanying.* London: National Society.

Jeffs, T (2003) Basil Henriques and the 'house of friendship' in Gilchrist, R, Jeffs, T and Spence, J (eds) *Architects of Change*. Leicester: Youth Work Press.

Klee, E, Dressen, W and Riess, V (1991) *Those were the days Holocaust through the eyes of perpetrators and bystanders.* London: Hamish Hamilton.

Klein, N (2000) *No logo*. London: Harper Collins.

Kohlberg, L (1981) *The philosophy of moral development*. San Francisco: Harper Row.

Kuchinke, K P (2001) Lawrence Kohlberg; in Palmer, J (ed) *Fifty modern thinkers.* London: Routledge.

Nietzsche, F (2002) *Beyond good and evil*. Cambridge: Cambridge University Press.

Piaget, J (1977) *The moral development of the child.* London: Penguin.

Power, F.C., Higgins, A., and Kohlberg, L (1989). *Lawrence Kohlberg's approach to moral education*. New York: Columbia University Press.

Roberts, J (2000) Practical ways for developing SMSC, in Best, R (2000) *Education for Spiritual, Moral, Social and Cultural Education*. London: Continuum.

Smith, L (2001) Jean Piaget, in Palmer, J (ed) *Fifty modern thinkers.* London: Routledge.

Welsh, I (1993) *Trainspotting*. London: Minerva.

WEBSITES

ARC (2007) Aktion Reinhard camps website www.Deathcamps.org

www.bbc.co.uk/ethics/

The internet is a good source of photographs as are the increasing number of museums.

The internet also gives quick access to government reports and primary legislation. Here are some examples related to animal welfare:

Animals Scientific Procedures Act 1986, **www.archive.official-documents.co.uk/document/hoc/321/321-xa.htm**

Burns Committee Report 2000, **www.defra.gov.uk/rural/hunting/inquiry/index.htm**

Hunting Act 2004, **www.opsi.gov.uk/ACTS/acts2004/ukpga_20040037_en_1**

Animal Welfare Act 2006, **www.opsi.gov.uk/acts/acts2006/pdf/ukpga_20060045_en.pdf**

Chapter 6
Youth workers and ethical conduct

CHAPTER OBJECTIVES

If you want to behave as a professional youth worker, this chapter will be the heart of the book. It is based on the National Youth Agency's (NYA) ethical code (2004) for youth workers. This code expresses the good things that all youth workers are committed to expressing in their professional practice. Earlier in the book we have thought about young people in society, and later we think about organising work, but here the focus in this chapter is on you as the youth worker.

Links to National and Professional Occupational Standards for Youth Work

Principle activity area	Examples of Units
5. Lead and manage teams and individuals	2.1.1, 2.3.1, 2.2.4, 2.4.1, 2.4.2, 4.2.7

The NYA ethical code

There are eight principles which divide into two types: those that set the direction and concerns for your face to face work with young people, and those that make sure you behave well as a professional in an organisation. I summarise the principles as:

1 respecting young people;

2 promoting young people's choices;

3 ensuring the welfare and safety of young people;

4 seeking social justice for young people;

5 keeping professional boundaries in your work;

6 being accountable for your work;

7 achieving competence in your work;

8 promoting ethical practice in your work.

Employers are inevitably worried about the second group (5–8) in case you bring their entire work into disrepute, and so you will hear a lot about these issues at induction and in job descriptions. But they are common concerns across all those who have jobs. What sets a youth worker apart is their core work, defined and expressed in the first group of principles (1–4): what good things you do in your relationships with and on behalf of young people. This chapter will go through each principle in turn, and will spend more time on each of those principles that focus on the young person, because that is where you will spend most of your time and effort at work. The NYA code also provides 'practice principles', they *relate more particularly to how the youth worker should act in the role of a practitioner . . .[they] are more specific, suggesting how youth workers would apply the broader ethical and professional principles. They are not exhaustive* (NYA, 2004). I shall quote the practice principles in each section, but will focus on the principle that youth workers are expected to express in their work.

Using the UN convention on the rights of the child

Youth workers are part of the international network of people who address the lives of 0–18 year olds. We are part of the commitment of the states who have signed up to the UN Convention on the Rights of the Child to provide services that conform to professional standards (UN Article 3.3). Those definitions of professional standards are in part informed by this international agreement, which in turn influences policy and legislation at a state level. Making the links between the NYA principles and the UN Convention on the Rights of the Child is important, can illuminate both and give an international status to youth work that is less susceptible to local variation. It can also avoid naive comments: when the Education and Inspections Act 2006 referred to parents some youth workers asked why: the preamble to the Convention sets the family as the *fundamental group of society* (paragraph 5).

Ethical principles that focus on the young person

1. Youth workers' commitment to treat young people with respect

This links to comments we have discussed about individuality and listening to young people.

What is respect?
'Respect' is a word that we should not pass over too quickly. I respect a young person when:

- I pay close attention to them;
- I direct my working time to them;
- I give them the highest value in my work (and life);
- they are my primary focus;
- I put them first.

Respecting young people as a focus of law and policy
This approach matches the underlying legislation and policy we work with.

- *The child is a person and not an object of concern* (Cleveland Inquiry, 1987, recommendation 2).

- UN Convention on the Rights of the Child Article 3: *the best interests of the child shall be the primary consideration* (1989).

- Climbié Inquiry (2003) recommendation 3: *work out how to implement the UN Convention on the Rights of the Child.*

- Every Child Matters (2004): *every child, not just some of them.*

Consequences of this priority for youth work
Respect means that the young people we work with are the absolute centre of the work we do, there is nothing and no one of more importance when setting priorities. We know them as unique individuals, each of significance and worth. Each young person's personal development will have a different character and require your professional attention. If you are in doubt about how to spend your time: spend it with a young person; that is what you are set apart to do. If you are wondering what to do with any resources: use them to benefit young people; you should be the first in the queue to argue their case at meetings of adults. Young people are our core activity and the purpose of our work.

A critical discussion of the NYA practice principles
Interestingly, the NYA ethics project reduced the scope of respect to a couple of rather negative themes: avoiding discrimination and managing information. These are certainly important issues for the employer worrying about equality and data protection legislation. But just focusing on them can pathologise the relationship between the youth worker and the young person. They also act as a 'presenting' characteristic of the young person rather than the person themselves: they become a black person to be treated fairly, or they become a vulnerable person because of the power of the information they give us. Finally they can move the focus from serving young people to being part of a complex organisation (a criticism raised by the Audit Commission in 2008 of the development of Children's Services since the Climbié Inquiry).

Practice principles would include:

- *valuing each young person and acting in a way that does not exploit or negatively discriminate against certain young people on irrelevant grounds such as 'race', religion, gender, ability or sexual orientation; and*

- *explaining the nature and limits of confidentiality and recognising that confidential information clearly entrusted for one purpose should not be used for another purpose without the agreement of the young person – except where there is clear evidence of danger to the young person, worker, other persons or the community.*

(NYA, 2004)

A critical discussion of the UN Convention on the Rights of the Child

The UN Convention raises several themes where the vulnerability of young person might need to be addressed. A youth worker may be the first professional who is aware of this vulnerability and can begin to advocate with and for the young person.

- Article 8 respects each child's right to their own identity, including: nationality, name and family relations. We might apply this to letting the young person define what they are called and not compel them to integrate or fit in.

- Article 16 protects each child from arbitrary interference with their privacy, family, home or correspondence; and unlawful attacks on their honour and reputation. We might apply this to bullying by their peers, and racial abuse and attacks. Would we also extend it to the excessive behaviour of targeted services?

- Article 21 links to Article 8 as it addresses adoption of children, including adoption across national boundaries. Youth workers may know the child well enough to hear about what is being practiced in secret. An Australian colleague reminds me of the historic placing out of young people by youth organisations as indentured servants under the guise of adoption, fostering and the care of orphans. Some of the practitioners are heroes of youth work: for example, in the 1850s, Lord Shaftesbury supported the St. Pancras Board of Guardians sending a small number of teenagers to the British West Indies, Barnardo sent 872 children to New South Wales in the 1920s.

- Article 25 focuses on giving periodic review of the care organised for young people. The risk for many teenagers in care is that time passes without a serious discussion about what will help them. Certainly there are meetings and minutes are taken but no real judgement is made and no action follows that makes a difference. The unspoken hope is that the young person will soon be old enough to be looked after by adult services, and so they are with a high proportion of long term prisoners having grown up looked after by professional carers (27 per cent of all prisoners and half of under 25 year olds in prison). Respecting young people means staying with them to achieve better long-term chances.

- Article 29 is about the development of the child's full potential through education. Respect here means that there ought to be the opportunity to study what will make the most of a young person's life and not to close down options.

- Article 30 addresses the particular issue of a child's native language. Use of a different language is a right, when it is exercised, that respects the difference and particular identity of an individual.

- Article 39 focuses on the recovery of children from torture, neglect and abuse. Respect here is to seek the health, self-respect and dignity of the child.

- Article 40 seeks the treatment of children by the law in ways that are fair and consistent with international law's treatment of adults.

ACTIVITY 6.1

Reflect on the priority you give young people.

- *How much time in the last week have you spent with young people?*

- *How much with other adults?*

- *Which of the UN articles link to issue you have faced? How?*

- *Write a short paragraph on the place you give to young people in your work.*

---

2. Youth workers' commitment to respect and to promote young people's rights to make their own decisions and choices; unless the welfare or legitimate interests of themselves or others are seriously threatened

This principle links to the comments about individual freedom and the competence of young people in decision making.

Defining the scope of young people's choices

It is up to youth workers to make sure that the choices young people want to make are top of the list in decision making. We looked at this earlier when thinking about participation. A youth worker will have a highly developed sense of the authenticity of young people's participation; they will be used to the decisions young people make and know quickly when an organisation or individual is manipulating or distorting the process. Youth workers collect different decision making tools and exercises so that they focus on the process that young people go through.

- Young people define the issue.

- Young people collect ideas.

- Young people check to include everyone.

- Young people debate the pros and cons.

- Young people make a judgement.

- Young people try out the decision.

- Young people review how it went.

- And maybe young people start all over again.

The contrast is clear: the process is the youth worker's task, the outcomes are the young people's – both their definition and achievement.

The NYA practice principles

The NYA project balances the practice of informal learning with the necessary input on the unforeseen and risky that professional adults need to contribute.

90

Practice principles would include:

- *raising young people's awareness of the range of decisions and choices open to them and offering opportunities for discussion and debate on the implications of particular choices;*

- *offering learning opportunities for young people to develop their capacities and confidence in making decisions and choices through participation in decision-making bodies and working in partnership with youth workers in planning activities;and*

- *respecting young people's own choices and views, unless the welfare or legitimate interests of themselves or other people are seriously threatened.*

(NYA, 2004)

ACTIVITY **6.2**

Discuss the following:

- *why could this list restrict a youth worker's intervention to giving information, advice and guidance?*

- *how do these principles promote the growth of lifelong learners?*

- *what would you add to encourage young people to take a bigger part in democratic society?*

The UN Convention on the Rights of the Child

The UN Convention also defines the child's rights to engage and contribute to public life, especially where they are at the heart of a decision. We discussed the issue of competence earlier: how far can young people be held responsible for 'adult' decisions'? The UN articles define competence in public settings in favour of the teenagers we work with. This is particularly true of the young person's 'voice', but also their independent creative and social behaviour – important aspects of youth work. Where there are weaknesses in the child's position a youth worker might be a suitable independent 'Lead professional' capable of supporting the child.

Here are five Articles that express these rights.

1 Article 12 states the right of the child to be heard in judicial and administrative processes.

2 Article 13 states the right to free expression.

3 Article 14 states a right to freedom of thought, conscience and religion.

4 Article 15 states the right to freedom of association and peaceful assembly.

5 Article 31 states the right to freedom of play, rest and leisure.

Freedom of choice

We have discussed the freedom of choice in a general way elsewhere. For young people to become effective adults in a democratic society they need to be capable of making their own mind up. Ethics for the youth worker is about making up your own mind and living in a world where not everything is precisely codified and regulated. Your work with young people is about making the space so that they can negotiate, choose, say no and yes, and be creative in an abundant life full of possibilities.

There are freedoms to choose even in health and safety

The area where there can be anxieties and fear of litigation in this process of making choices is 'health and safety'. We will return to this in the next section, but here I want to draw attention to the importance of allowing young people to make a choice.

CASE STUDY

Case study of Law Lords judgment (2004) Tomlinson vs Congleton.

18-year-old John Tomlinson broke his neck swimming in Congleton District Council's country park one sunny Bank Holiday. A series of court cases tested the liability of the council and sought damages for the, now, paraplegic young man. The case went to the Law Lords for a judgment. Should the council have had better signs? Closed off the beach? Installed lifeguards?

Here are some of the Law Lords' judgments.

Lord Hoffmann
- *39. According to the Royal Society for the Prevention of Accidents, . . .about 25–35 [young men a year] break their necks diving . . .there is obviously some degree of risk in swimming and diving, as there is in climbing, cycling, fell walking and many other such activities.*

- *42. The Court of Appeal made no reference at all to the social value of the activities which were to be prohibited. The majority of people who went to the beaches to sunbathe, paddle and play with their children were enjoying themselves in a way which gave them pleasure and caused no risk to themselves or anyone else. This must be something to be taken into account in deciding whether it was reasonable to expect the Council to destroy the beaches.*

- *45. I think it will be extremely rare for an occupier of land to be under a duty to prevent people from taking risks which are inherent in the activities they freely choose to undertake upon the land. If people want to climb mountains, go hang gliding or swim or dive in ponds or lakes that is their affair.*

Lord Scott of Foscote
- *94. He [Tomlinson] was simply sporting about in the water with his friends, giving free rein to his exuberance. And why not? And why should the Council be discouraged by the*

CASE STUDY *continued*

law of tort from providing facilities for young men and young women to enjoy themselves in this way? Of course there is some risk of accidents arising out of the joie de vivre of the young. But that is no reason for imposing a grey and dull safety regime on everyone.

ACTIVITY **6.3**

Prepare advice for the council on the use of public parks so that young people can choose freely in their own time what they do.

3. Youth workers' commitment to promote and ensure the welfare and safety of young people, while permitting them to learn through undertaking challenging educational activities

This links to earlier discussions of association and learning.

Defining the scope of this principle

High expectations on the adults who work with young people and high expectations of the achievements of young people are at the heart of Every Child Matters. The welfare, safety and learning of young people connect with deep roots in youth work practice. Early practitioners were committed to the 'rescue' of young people from the circumstances of their lives: poverty, drunkenness, ignorance, or life as orphans with no adult to stand up for them. The neighbourhood renewal projects of the last decade have reinforced this public concern to address the restrictions placed on young people's lives by poverty. The genius of youth work that developed (particularly due to the ideas of Baden-Powell and Hahn) was to increase the extent of the challenge given to the young people. The Albemarle report placed challenge alongside association and training as the three key notes of the youth service. If association seems to focus on the young person's interest, and training on the adults' concerns; challenge is needed to: *capture their enthusiasm and to ensure the fullest development of their qualities of mind and body. . .satisfying the sense of achievement for which all hunger and which so many have failed to find in school or work* (Albemarle Report, 1960, p61). Challenge was defined by examples of outdoor physical adventure, travel, volunteering, cultural activities in the club.

Historical memorials

This combination of improving the welfare of young people and opening the doors to new challenges is rightly celebrated in memorials to youth workers. Some are formal public statues: the bronze mounted on a stone plinth in the middle of Portland Place showing

Quintin Hogg in a 'Ragged School' teaching boys to read. It is quite a contrast: his formal Victorian clothes, their rags; the public monument in Nash's elegant London, his work in London's alleys, yards and slums. Others are less public: the plaque on a bench outside Black Sail Youth Hostel in Ennerdale to GN 'Flash' Birch who brought Leeds children to climb Great Gable between 1945 and 1991. These are great memorials because they express the gratitude of the young people who were changed by the excellent commitment of the adults, and they recognise in public the good that is created by this work.

Anxieties about risks

The prevailing tone (reflected here in the odd idea of 'permitting' young people to learn) of recent discussion has been to emphasise the health and safety duties. This is in part justified. The Lyme Bay disaster of 1993 when four teenagers died kayaking in the English Channel was full of things that went wrong: bad assessments of risk and of setting, weak support, inadequate preparation for emergencies, unqualified staff, and so on. It was quite right that the report into the event created the system of the Adventure Activities Licensing Authority (AALA) and the linking of licensing to National Governing Body Awards (see principle 7: competence), so that managers of groups and parents of young people can know if it is likely that their child will be safe (see principle 6: accountability). But you can see from the way I have included principles 6 and 7 that the 'welfare and safety of young people' doesn't just mean the carrying out the health and safety duties. Best practice is achieved by applying all three ethical principles.

Risk, welfare and safety of young people are much wider than just the 'health and safety' requirements. The person who is to be the beneficiary of this principle is the young person. The young person may be at risk of abuse at the hands of others, but in situations where there are no dangers caused by the planned activity of the youth worker. The young person's welfare may be at risk because of not finding a suitable foster placement to take them from local authority care, or because a parent wishes to take them illicitly from their home overseas; but in each case there may be no 'health and safety' practical risk.

A critical discussion of the UN Convention on the Rights of the Child

Examples from the UN Convention of welfare and risk issues to be addressed.

- Article 11: the risks of the illicit transfer of children between countries.

- Article 19: the risks of 'the physical or mental violence, injury or abuse, neglect or negligent treatment, maltreatment or exploitation, including sexual abuse' (cf Article 34).

- Article 24: the right to the highest possible health: addressing disease, malnutrition, poor water and sanitation, and promoting breast feeding.

- Article 26: the right to social security benefits.

- Article 27: the right to a standard of living adequate for the child's physical, mental, spiritual, moral and social development.

- Article 28: in considering the right to education, includes the state's duties to encourage regular school attendance and reduce drop out rates.

- Article 32: the risks of economic exploitation and their affects on the education and whole development of the child.

- Article 33: the risks of the illicit use of narcotic drugs and psychotropic substances.

- Article 35: the risks of the abduction or sale or trafficking of children.

All the examples from the UN list focus on the risk to the child from events and activities often undertaken by individuals other than those employed to act in the public good. These rights suggest that youth workers should be engaged in transformational work to challenge the unjust behaviour of adults towards young people by providing welfare and safety.

A critical discussion of the NYA practice principles
The boundaries of the NYA project's seem smaller than this.

Practice principles would include:

- *taking responsibility for assessing risk and managing the safety of work and activities involving young people;*

- *ensuring their own competence, and that of employees and volunteers for whom they are responsible, to undertake areas of work and activities;*

- *warning the appropriate authority, and taking action, if there are thought to be risks or dangers attached to the work;*

- *drawing to the attention of their employer and, if this proves ineffective, bringing to the attention of those in power or, finally, the general public, ways in which activities or policies of employers may be seriously harmful to the interests and safety of young people; and*

- *being aware of the need to strike a balance between avoiding unnecessary risk and permitting and encouraging young people to partake in challenging educational activities.*

(NYA, 2004)

ACTIVITY 6.4

Suggest ways of providing welfare and safety in addition to the NYA list.

---

4. Youth workers' commitment to contribute towards the promotion of social justice for young people and in society generally, through encouraging respect for difference and diversity and challenging discrimination

Practice principles would include:

- *promoting just and fair behaviour, and challenging discriminatory actions and attitudes on the part of young people, colleagues and others;*

- encouraging young people to respect and value difference and diversity, particularly in the context of a multi-cultural society;

- drawing attention to unjust policies and practices and actively seeking to change them;

- promoting the participation of all young people, and particularly those who have traditionally been discriminated against, in youth work, in public structures and in society generally; and

- encouraging young people and others to work together collectively on issues of common concern.

(NYA, 2004)

This principle is focused on the role of youth workers in facilitating groups. It picks up from the earlier discussions of equality, association, and the moral development of young people. It has two types of activity: a positive action to achieve social justice and an action to prevent injustice. It expects this commitment to be expressed in two areas: the direct work done with young people, and the wider society.

ACTIVITY 6.5

Give examples of each expression of this principle.

	Achieve social justice	Action to prevent injustice
Work done with young people		
Wider society		

Why is social justice important for youth work?

Chapter 3 explored themes of equality and social justice. In Chapter 2 we looked at association: real association that sets a standard for the fair and inclusive society will need action by youth workers to ensure that everyone can take part.

This principle is all about the social development of young people. It balances the personal focus of the 'respect' principle with a concern for the wider society which the young people are part of. It moderates the libertarian free-for-all of choice with the legal requirements and the sense of natural justice that seeks fairness rather than abuse of the minority or the weak. It also sets the welfare, safety and challenge elements of a learning process within a tolerant, inclusive society that lives with difference and prefers thoughtful, accountable action to prejudice.

Why does social justice have a concern wider than the practice of youth work?

Connecting what happens inside youth work with the wider social justice debates outside, in wider society, may seem a bit unreasonable: surely youth work is enough? The connection reflects the unity of justice: it does not matter who you are, it applies to all so that it can be fair. This connection also makes sense of the transparency of action of the youth worker: it will not make sense to the young people for you to challenge racism and try to include black and white in the youth centre in your work, and for you to be marching with racists to stir up hatred in your spare time. Whatever you intend, fairness and transparency will require consistency across your life.

Achieving social justice as part of a progressive society

Promoting social justice as a core activity places youth workers at the heart of a progressive society. Changing attitudes, for example, to the poor (UN Article 27), the poorly educated (UN Article 28), refugees (UN Article 22), the disabled (UN Article 23), is to take on a difficult social argument that goes against the flow of money, learning, status, and physical and mental abilities. But the rightness of the position is seen in the networks, organisations, campaigns, and legislation that also work to achieve these ends. Unity of purpose can produce encouragement (you are not the only one doing this) and support (here are arguments and activities that work). Good youth workers have taken a lead in social inclusion programmes in the UK such as the New Deal for Communities and the National Strategy for Neighbourhood Renewal: their practice of the core value of social justice has prepared them for complex holistic programmes tackling multiple deprivation.

Power disputes and beneficiaries of unfair societies

Some of the rich and powerful prefer to hang on to their position by paying people to moan about 'political correctness (gone mad)' as part of the reaction to any progress that can be made in achieving greater equality and fairness. Youth workers have their efforts to be inclusive met with this common argument, so what can we do to respond?

Firstly: it is important to recognise whose interests are served by this argument. Changing the balance of power, as we try to do, between girls and boys; black and white will annoy the powerful who benefit from the previous arrangements.

Secondly: assess how the powerful benefit: grotesque laddish jokes benefit men by preparing young women as sexual servants, limiting the social status and competence of the disabled reduces competition in the work place.

Thirdly: dissect the extent to which this is a matter of the public or private sphere. 'Political correctness' in part expresses the invasion of the private sphere by public policy and sets a battle line to 'roll back the frontier of the state'. This is a genuinely difficult area. The UN Convention preamble includes a reference to families (3) because many of the Articles express the reasons for the States to enter the private life of families to protect children. Powerful people object to having their power challenged, but the very characteristic of power is that it affects other people and is not private in either its intentions or consequences. Youth workers are quite clear that we work for the public benefit. When you are challenged: look at the public effect of the objector.

Ethical principles that focus on the workplace

5. Youth workers' commitment to recognise the boundaries between personal and professional life and be aware of the need to balance a caring and supportive relationship with young people with appropriate professional distance

Practice principles would include:

- *recognising the tensions between developing supportive and caring relationships with young people and the need to maintain an appropriate professional distance;*

- *taking care not to develop close personal, particularly sexual, relationships with the young people they are working with as this may be against the law, exploitative or result in preferential treatment. If such a relationship does develop, the youth worker concerned should report this to the line manager to decide on appropriate action;*

- *not engaging in work-related activities for personal gain, or accepting gifts or favours from young people or local people that may compromise the professional integrity of the work; and*

- *taking care that behaviour outside work does not undermine the confidence of young people and the public in youth work.*

(NYA, 2004)

The quest for commitment

Anne Foreman asked youth workers 'Are we really to stop giving young people a hug?' and was met with loud applause (Eagles Wings, 1993). Youth workers use all sorts of communication to make it clear to young people that they are their first concern. Some object to the idea of being friends with young people: it smacks of something for our own benefit or pleasure; or an activity for the private rather than professional sphere. Aristotle would agree that it should be for the sake of the friend and not our own benefit. From that we need to have authentic relationships, as Neal Terry says: *The relationship is everything because personal growth, development, learning about values, are human tasks that can only be done within a relationship* (Young, 1999, p62).

The need to manage yourself

Boundaries are about restraint. Certainly we are enthusiastic, energetic; attracting young people to take part; but we are able to stop and think, to plan and act even handedly, to be fair to the range of young people we work with. Being an adolescent is not always an attractive prospect to adults and yet youth workers need to be fair to all those they work with, not just the easy, pleasant or attractive ones. The ancient vows of poverty, chastity and obedience seem to be only for people with strange habits, but all three address money, sex, and power which are the heart of the risks that youth workers face in managing themselves for effective practice. Failing to manage the boundaries in the areas of sex and money are understandable causes of scandal that bring youth work into disrepute, but the abuse of power is just as devastating for the young people.

Money

More youth workers lose their jobs and reputations over money than anything else: funders don't trust the credibility of the organisation; stakeholders withdraw their support; and sometimes people go to prison. The main boundary here is the one between the worker's money and the youth work money and it needs to be kept absolutely clear. The work is done for the public benefit and there will be various systems that express this: Local Authority management systems; charity accounting practice; and so on. The best projects have separate staff with responsibility for finance. Here are seven basic rules to help maintain the boundary.

1 Keep money that comes in, and money that goes out separate in a written record – buy and use a cash book.

2 Always give receipts for money – in ink, from a numbered duplicate book.

3 Always get receipts for money paid out.

4 Pay surplus cash in to a bank account.

5 Have clear procedures for receiving cash.

6 Restrict access to the petty cash, for example have a lockable cash box.

7 Keep cash transactions to a minimum.

Sex and intimacy

Sexual intimacy can be presented as a contested subject in young people's lives. Sex workers and their rights can be placed in opposition to the objectification of women which creates prejudice. Young people are developing their personal relationship skills and these will include sex; on the other hand young people are vulnerable, exploited and at risk. This debate was used by some male youth workers a generation ago to justify relationships with young people and younger workers that we know are unacceptable. For youth workers there should be no ambiguity: the sexual relationships must fall into those categories of pleasure and utility for the youth worker that Aristotle is so critical of. If you want to get sexual pleasure or usefully procreate then do it away from the job and not with the people you are meant to serve. Manage your own desires, and in the process you are likely to help keep young people safe.

Boundaries are also a clear issue when we consider adults including their own children in a youth group. Most good practice would say that in such cases the effectiveness of the parent or guardian to act as a professional for the whole group is impaired and any staff to young people ratio can not include them. The reason is that, despite the best intentions, in a crisis the parent will naturally focus on their child above all others. This point was tragically illustrated when Patricia Palmer, an education support assistant, took her son Max with the school trip to the Lake District; she was helping staff. Unwise plunge pooling by unqualified staff (see Chapter 7 for more on the responsibilities of manager and worker to ensure the competence) at Glenridding Beck in spate led to the mother risking her life for her child who was dying in the water. What we might do with our family – knowing their capacity and resilience – is not the same as we can do in a group where we will not know how they will respond, particularly in unfamiliar conditions.

Power

Restraint is about the power needs of the adult. The Cullen Inquiry 1996 reported on the killing of primary school children and staff at Dunblane and is mainly remembered for firearms control and better security arrangements in schools. But Thomas Hamilton was also a persistent organiser of youth groups and the recommendations include the vetting of those who organise voluntary clubs and a qualification for such volunteers, CRB checks, and the S/NVQs in Youth Work can now meet those requirements (Cullen, 1996, 12, p27–28). The interesting aspect of the report is the ability of the voluntary sector (the Scouts) to ban Hamilton from acting in their name when it became clear that he was not able to maintain a boundary between the care of the lads (risking hypothermia at least) and his own *delusions of grandeur* (Cullen, 1996, 4 p4–8). On the other hand: for 16 years he ran voluntary groups attached to public bodies such as schools and there was no real effective prevention despite complaints (Cullen, 1996, 4 p9–63). The report repays careful reading by the voluntary youth service, and by those commissioning or working in partnership with it (Cullen, 1996, p11).

ACTIVITY 6.6

- *What are the boundary lines that you can see in your work from the areas identified and discussed here?*

- *Write yourself rules to mark the boundary you will not cross.*

- *Discuss and improve your list.*

---

6. Youth workers' commitment to recognise the need to be accountable to young people, their parents or guardians, colleagues, funders, wider society and others with a relevant interest in the work, and that these accountabilities may be in conflict

Practice principles would include:

- *recognising that accountabilities to different groups may conflict and taking responsibility for seeking appropriate advice and making decisions in cases of conflict;*

- *being open and honest in all dealings with young people, enabling them to access information to make choices and decisions in their lives generally and in relation to participation in youth work activities;*

- *ensuring that actions as a youth worker are in accordance with the law;*

- *ensuring that resources under youth workers' control are distributed fairly, according to criteria for which youth workers are accountable, and that work undertaken is as effective as possible;*

- *reporting to the appropriate authority any suspicions relating to a young person being at risk of serious harm or danger, particularly of sexual or physical abuse; and*

- *actively seeking opportunities to collaborate with colleagues and professionals from other agencies.*

(NYA, 2004)

The youth work that began Chapter 2 identifies a series of stakeholders. This principle expects the youth worker to be able to articulate arguments to the different interest groups about the youth work that is planned, or has taken place. Youth work places itself as an activity that is of public benefit and the more complicated the interest groups the more complex the types of accountability become.

Accountability in voluntary small projects
Perhaps the simplest youth work will involve volunteer youth workers and no money changing hands.

Youth workers will be accountable to the young people who come. This will be expressed in the programme planning and evaluation and the young people will respond with comments, ideas and by choosing to be there.

Youth workers will also be accountable to the parents of the young people. Under 18s are not completely free to make their own choices and the parents will need to know what is planned, give permission, and being well enough informed about the staff competence to consent.

Youth workers will not work alone and will therefore need to be accountable to each other. In practice this means planning the session together, carrying out what has been agreed, and evaluating how it went.

Accountability in youth work projects with budgets
There are not many examples of youth work where no money changes hands. Very quickly there is a tea fund, or cash to buy tickets on a trip out, or regular subscription. In his early campaigns Gandhi set the tone of public benefit and accountability by insisting on meticulous care for any money. Youth workers need to do the same. Separate accounts, careful recording of money, safe keeping of cash and regular public statements reviewing the money are essential with even the smallest amounts. It must be absolutely clear that the youth worker is only handling any money to benefit the work and not themselves (this links to principle 5 about boundaries). Money is such a cause of scandal that all the dealings need to be subjected to competent and independent scrutiny by someone who will think through how the money has been used and check the account given by the project. Ideally youth workers will have someone else who deals with the money to reduce the risks to the reputation of their work, but this is not always practical.

Accountability in youth work that is part of wider networks
Plenty of youth work has grown up in networks which provide common advice, guidance, and patterns of working. The Scout leader who reads Policy, Organisation and Rules is trying to connect their group with the millions of other Scouts across the world. Accountability certainly means completing returns to the headquarters, but it also means checking to see whether your own practice matches best practice in the network. Revisions of guidance, awards, and minimum requirements; updating qualifications; taking part in regional and

101

national meetings are all ways in which accountability is expressed to others who are committed to this type of work. The importance of the accountability to specialist colleagues is clear if you attend these meetings. Networks for detached youth work, black workers, and so on are places of passionate debate as we try to improve what we do.

Accountability in local authority youth work

Accountability reaches new audiences for local authority workers. The ward councillors where you work will have particular concerns. National policy and its local implementation will mean that your explanations and plans need to line up with what else has been planned. Perhaps the best plan is to work out how you can contribute to strategic targets from your work, before you are given targets that have become unrelated to your work.

Accountability in partnership youth work

Many of us work in partnerships. Accountability here means all of the above plus information sharing, planning, teamwork, coordination and evaluation with other agencies. A real understanding of the partner's main purpose is crucial if you are going to be accountable to them in a way that will make any sense to them. The Health Authority is interested in the health of young people; the Police in crime; the Fire and Rescue Service in arson; and so on. You do need to talk about youth work to the young people, other youth workers, and your managers. But these partners need to see how what you do together makes their work better. Too many people are spending too much time in partnership meetings avoiding the decision to work with young people.

Meetings

Accountability does mean meetings. Those meetings need to be well enough prepared to avoid them being a fraud. Reports do need to be written. They need to be clear and linked to what you promised to do. They need to go out in time for people to read them before the meeting. The range of people who are typically part of these meetings is inevitably wide, so planning dates and sticking to them is an important part of being reliable. Reliability is probably the most important characteristic of being accountable.

7. Youth workers' commitment to develop and maintain the required skills and competence to do the job

Practice principles would include:

- *only undertaking work or taking on responsibilities for which workers have the necessary skills, knowledge and support;*

- *seeking feedback from service users and colleagues on the quality of their work and constantly updating skills and knowledge; and*

- *recognising when new skills and knowledge are required and seeking relevant education and training.*

(NYA, 2004)

Youth workers are educated

Youth work is a skilled and learned profession and, though people are drawn into it in different ways, it can't be done for long or to any level of real competence unless the workers learn and quality. Volunteers and peer mentors at the entry point to the profession need thoughtful and effective learning for their roles to make any sense to themselves and the young people. A worker who is not inducted and trained has not entered the role of youth worker but remains a service user, drawing from and unsure how to contribute to the organisation.

Youth work is educational

Youth work is a profession that values learning and development. We find it easier to convince its beneficiaries that we value learning, changing, being willing to be assessed – and live with the need for reassessment. Progressive and linked learning within youth work is an essential part of the accountability of youth workers within the profession as well as being developmental for individuals and the capacity of organisations and neighbourhoods. Making time for your own learning and the learning of colleagues makes your work more efficient as you find clearer ways of working and build better teams to tackle the work. New areas of work open up and more explicit qualifications replace the university of life. You will need to be assessed in areas you have been doing for years, and you will need to learn new things to maintain currency of service to young people and accountability to all the stakeholders.

Youth work develops by learning

Youth work values reflection as central to learning. Supervision and observation of competence by colleagues is part of this and needs to be part of the qualifications we do. Reflection on practice by the young people we work with also needs to be built in. Clearly this is because we place young people's voices at the heart of our work, giving them power in determining the nature of the service. It is also possible to hear in young people's comments feedback which may not be so filtered by euphemism.

Planning youth work staffing requirements

Taking on new work requires thought in terms of resources. The most critical resource will be the capacity of the people to do the work. Typically the discussion asks these questions.

- How many competent people will be needed?

- What are the competences required?

- How are those expressed as qualifications?

- Is it likely that we will be able to recruit all the staff we will need with those qualifications?

The next stage is to draw a person specification to match the task. I use the layout in Table 6.1.

Table 6.1 Person specification for the task

Tasks	Desirable competences and qualifications	Essential competences and qualifications

---

ACTIVITY 6.7

Suggest a person specification to work in a team of three youth workers who are going to undertake detached youth work on an estate where there are particular concerns about anti-social behaviour, and teenage pregnancy. Justify the choices you make about the different tasks you identify and the difference between essential and desirable.

Capacity problems in recruitment

In some of the most deprived communities it has proved difficult to recruit staff. One reaction to this is to re-advertise and delay the project. This is a risky strategy as it may produce no better response and only delays delivery of a service to young people that is known to be important. An alternative that has been used to good effect is to have a plan B.

Plan B

Look at the person specification that you produced in Table 6.1. Which qualification is both essential and likely to be a stumbling block? (such as NVQ 2 Youth Work)

Write a second person specification for a trainee post and include the learning, assessment and qualification (and a time deadline for this to be achieved) as a task. If the post is paid it could not fairly be offered at the same rate as a qualified worker; and wise projects would use the balance of the cash to pay for the learning. Clearly once the trainee has the qualification they then meet the competence required for the proper job and they should take up that contract and that level on the pay scale.

8. Youth workers' commitment to work for conditions in employing agencies where these principles are discussed, evaluated and upheld. Foster and engage in ethical debate in youth work

Practice principles would include:

- *developing awareness of youth workers' own personal values and how these relate to the ethical principles of youth work;*

- *re-examining these principles, engaging in reflection and discussion with colleagues and contributing to the learning of the organisation where they work;*

- *developing awareness of the potential for conflict between personal and professional values, as well as between the interests and rights of different individuals and between the ethical principles in this statement; and*

- *recognising the importance of continuing reflection and debate and seeing this statement of ethical principles as a working document which should be constantly under discussion.*

- *ensuring that colleagues, employers and young people are aware of the statement of principles;*

- *being prepared to discuss difficult ethical issues in the light of these principles and contributing towards interpreting and elaborating on the practice principles; and*

- *being prepared to challenge colleagues or employing agencies whose actions or policies are contrary to the principles in this statement.*

- *The opportunities and necessity of discussing and reviewing practice to ensure that good youth work is sustained.*

(NYA, 2004)

Who do we discuss ethics with?

Regular supervision of youth work allows you to manage ethical complexity and ambiguity. Michael Carroll identified four stages for ethical decision making.

1 *Creating ethical sensitivity: what impact does your behaviour have on others? What are the principles?*

2 *Formulating a course of action: talk through the facts and values.*

3 *Implementing the ethical decision: carry out the plan.*

4 *Living with the ambiguities of the ethical decision: deal with doubt and uncertainty.*

(Hawkins and Shohet, 2000, p47ff)

Youth workers who stay with the work for the long term organise regular meetings for supervision (often outside the work setting). They talk through a dilemma and will meet up every month or six weeks to reflect on ethics. This personal level is fundamental to professional practice.

Next we discuss ethics where we are working as part of the design, planning, evaluation, and report of the work. This will mean in team meetings and in management meetings.

Finally, on the basis that youth work is doing a good thing in society, we also discuss, explain, and advocate our principles with the wider population. We need to do this so that people know what we do all day, to be accountable and to gain support.

How do we organise to discuss ethics?

One purpose of this book is to make it clear that ethical debate is strongly linked to all aspects of youth work practice: the choices we make in youth work are expressions of values and some of the arguments we have are genuine dilemmas where different values have to be balanced. I hope that at least some of the arguments, examples, and questions will provoke conversations in your work place. I hope that in the future you will come back to this book and think about what is happening using this discussion.

ACTIVITY **6.8**

What have you read about so far that needs to be talked through with young people, colleagues, or managers?

When do we discuss ethics?

Regularly is the inevitable answer. But different time cycles will work for different discussions. A monthly cycle will work well for a local project that meets for planning and management purposes. Reviewing individual sessions will mean that each session might include an ethical discussion as part of the review and planning.

Longer cycles are useful for national networks, and defining codes or qualification requirements. So, six monthly or annual conferences are an important aspect of professional up dating as it allows you to put your work alongside that of others from very different settings. That contrast of context can help highlight the common values of youth work. But too much discussion away from your context during the year will not help the development of context–mechanism–outcome configurations which we will discuss later (Pawson and Tilley, 1997). Again, qualification and competence definitions require complex consultation to get them right. They then need time to be used so that there is sufficient understanding of them working normally after the initial shock of working out how the new definitions fit with what we already know. If the iterations to improve are too quick there is a sense that no one knows what is going on, if they are too slow: no one listens. So the change cycle tends to be about every five years.

ACTIVITY **6.9**

Review activity

- *Look at the full text for the NYA Ethical code on the website.*

- *Investigate supervision or review your own supervision arrangements to include insights about ethics.*

- *Read: Hawkins and Shohet (2000) Chapter 3, Getting the supervision you need.*

C H A P T E R   R E V I E W

The development of ethical reflection changes the practice and structures of youth work. We make a new artifice to ensure that our practice that is good can be encouraged and that the bad practice is more difficult to maintain. Ethical reflection is transformative for the profession. This chapter will have helped you make sense of each element of the ethical code for yourself. Chapter 9 will give some worked examples of how you might use the code in complex settings. The code is important, but clearly there are other ways of expressing our values.

EFERENCES

Cullen Inquiry (1996) *The public inquiry into the shootings at Dunblane Primary School on 13 March 1996*. London: The Stationery Office.

DfES (2004) *Every child matters*. London: Department for Education and Skills.

Hawkins, P and Shohet, R (2000) *Supervision in the helping professions*. Maidenhead: Open University Press.

Laming Report (2003) *The Victoria Climbié Inquiry*. London: The Stationery Office.

NYA (1999) Ethical conduct in youth work, in Harrison, R and Wise, C (2005) *Working with young people*. London: Sage.

Pawson, R and Tilley, N (1997) *Realistic evaluation*. London: Sage.

Young, K (1999) *The art of youth work*. Lyme Regis: Russell House Publishing.

WEBSITES

Audit Commission (2008) Are we there yet? Improving governance and resource management in Children's Trusts **www.auditcommission.gov.uk/childrenstrusts/report.pdf**

Education and Inspections Act 2006 The full Act is available on the internet at **www.opsi.gov.uk/ACTS/acts2006/ukpga_20060040_en_2#pt1-l1g6**

Every Child Matters 2004 **www.everychildmatters.gov.uk/**

United Nations (1989) Convention for the Rights of the Child **www.unicef.org/crc/**

Chapter 7

Youth work organisations as ethical projects

CHAPTER OBJECTIVES

This chapter is for all who design and manage youth work projects. Youth work organisations, however modest, are trying to carry out ethical insights (Chapters 2–4). The nature of working together means that other ethical questions arise. Here are the four broad areas we will look at.

1 What do we prioritise?

2 How do we relate to the parents of the young people, and the others who live in the area?

3 How do we explain what we have been doing with our time and money?

4 How do we ensure a reliable and trustworthy way of working in changing circumstances?

Applying values in the public sphere can scorned as politically correct, do-gooding, god-bothering, patronising, philanthropy. Certainly, as you read this chapter there will be some approaches that you may not be attracted by and some values that you may find odd and alien. But the invitation in youth work is to find broad alliances of values and to seek common purpose in the service of young people. I am encouraged by this reassertion of the importance of expressing values in the public sphere.

Now there are some who question the scale of our ambitions. . . Their memories are short. For they have forgotten what this country [we might say 'youth work'] has already done; what free men and women can achieve when imagination is joined to common purpose, and necessity to courage.

(Obama, 2009)

These questions will be important for those who work using the Professional and National Occupational Standards for Youth Work.

Links to the first level functions and the related units

Principle activity area	Examples of Units
3 work with others	1.2.2, 1.2.3, 2.1.1, 2.2.3, 2.3.2,
4 develop youth work strategy and practice	2.4.1, 2.4.2, 3.1.1, 3.2.1, 3.3.3,
5 Lead and manage teams and individuals	4.1.1, 4.1.2, 4.2.1, 4.2.2, 4.2.6,
	4.4.1, 4.4.2, 5.2.2, 5.2.3, 5.4.1

They also relate to the following youth work values.

- It recognises, respects and is actively responsive to the wider networks of peers, communities, families, and cultures which are important to young people, and through these networks seeks to help young people to achieve stronger relationships and collective identities, through the promotion of inclusivity.

- It works in partnership with young people and other agencies which contribute to young people's social, educational and personal development.

- It safeguards the welfare of young people, and provides them with a safe environment in which to explore their values, beliefs, ideas and issues.

(NOS, 2008:4)

The establishment of organisations to express an ethical purpose among young people

Responding to the needs of particular groups of young people is a constantly changing activity: finding ways of working to address the current assessment of need requires thought.

Types of origins

Youth work projects do not all start in the same way and they are not all maintained and supported in the same way. I distinguish between those that have emerged locally and those that are extensions of networks of practice.

The emergence of local projects to address local perceived needs among young people

The good that is expressed here is that we will do something with and for the young people. The conversations that will have been had are:

- we want to. . .;

- we've nowhere to go;

- I'd like somewhere for them to meet;

- they need something worthwhile to do.

The conversations lead to a meeting.

- How can the young people take their idea forward?

- Who do we need to involve?

- Where can we get support for resources?

- What would be a good way of organising things?

- How do we staff the sessions?

The meeting makes a plan. The plan is organised as minutes and the minutes are checked. The plan becomes a budget, and a staffing rota. With help from the CVS, the plan becomes a constitution.

The organisation divides the work between those who'll work directly with young people and those who will back them up, provide the resources, encouragement and support.

A management group has important ethical roles.

- The treasurer allows the financial control to be separated from the worker, but this is probably best thought of as accountability.

- The secretary allows the supporting bureaucracy of keeping records and ensuring communication to the stakeholders not to burden the worker. This is also best thought of as accountability.

- The chair focuses the board's role as an ethical enterprise. The chair:

   - ensures that the organisation delivers to the people it serves;

   - leads the organisation;

   - leads the key workers and makes space for them to achieve;

   - consults and listens widely, and then takes people with them;

   - through consultation and listening decides the organisation's strategy and culture;

   - sets the pace of the organisation;

   - sets priorities (and non-priorities);

   - monitors progress, check it happens, but doesn't do it;

   - celebrates achievement.

(Petit-Zeman, 2006, p2ff)

The practice of ethical leadership is disclosed in this list by the character of the organisation and the dialogues. Youth projects tend to be not-for-profit organisations rather than businesses or straightforward public administrations. They can be argued to be more influenced by environmental changes in both values and social standards, and socio-economic factors. Economic factors will affect business more, and political change will affect public administration more (Vernis et al., 2006, p2). This social and moral role is reinforced by the placing of non-profit organisations in society between families, the state, and the market (Evers and Wintersberger in Vernis et al., 2006, p3). The challenge of working out how to express the project's responses to the ethical context is the central task for the leaders of a local project.

The use of networks to spread the good practices of a particular approach to youth work

Networks are a common way of youth work practice spreading. We see good practice in the paper or on the news and say *we should do that here*. The publication of ideas (for example by George Williams for the YMCA, or Maude Stanley for girls clubs), and, above all, rationales for the type of work allows local groups to try them out. Organisations may be called upon by local activists to respond to a need, contribute support, or provide training and quality support to launch and validate the work.

The examples I have given so far might give the impression that this is just for the voluntary sector, but Local Authorities work this way too. A group of local activists might campaign for some youth work in their area, working with elected members and officers to justify the case; if it is agreed there may be conditions:

* standard quality systems;

* training and competence based assessment for local volunteers;

* agreements about review of progress against agreed results.

With the increased commissioning of services and the need to achieve outcomes for Children's Services it is likely that this will be the common way of working. Networks allow good practice to be applied in a new setting; some off the peg solutions are enough for what is required, they also allow shared support in the development of new practice, for example the development of the 'Young Advisors' has enabled new learning about young people giving advice to public services.

The nature of need

Education and Inspections Act 2006 (c. 40) Part 1 – Education functions of local authorities (Functions in respect of youth work, recreation, etc).

507B LEAs in England: functions in respect of leisure-time activities etc. for persons aged 13 to 19 and certain persons aged 20 to 24.

1 A local education authority in England must, so far as reasonably practicable, secure for qualifying young persons in the authority's area access to:

a sufficient educational leisure-time activities which are for the improvement of their well-being, and sufficient facilities for such activities; and

b sufficient recreational leisure-time activities which are for the improvement of their well-being, and sufficient facilities for such activities.

2 Qualifying young persons, for the purposes of this section, are:

a persons who have attained the age of 13 but not the age of 20; and

b persons who have attained the age of 20 but not the age of 25 and have a learning difficulty (within the meaning of section 13(5)(a) and (6) of the Learning and Skills Act 2000).

3 For the purposes of subsection (1)(a):

a sufficient educational leisure-time activities which are for the improvement of the well-being of qualifying young persons in the authority's area must include sufficient educational leisure time activities which are for the improvement of their personal and social development, and

b sufficient facilities for such activities must include sufficient facilities for educational leisure-time activities which are for the improvement of the personal and social development of qualifying young persons in the authority's area.

Task: answer these questions.

• Who has lead responsibility for assessing need?

• What is the central purpose of leisure time activities for the age group?

• Which aspects of youth work are measures of sufficient resources to meet young people's needs?

Evidence

Agreeing what needs to be done for young people is like much else in the public domain: it needs to be backed up by sound evidence. When the National Strategy for Neighbourhood Renewal began, Policy Action Team (PAT) 18 worked on the persistent problem for neighbourhood action: better information (PAT18, 2000). Why does better information matter? Here are some problems caused by not having adequate data.

• Ignorance and inattention: policy makers don't know the scale and location of problems.

• Therefore they neglect inequalities, such as the high extent of the Black and Minority Ethnic population in the most deprived areas.

• Policies get misdirected or mistargeted: wasting money in one area and not spending it where it is needed, allowing inequalities in spending and action.

• Trends and developing patterns get missed, until there is a surprise national crisis.

• Communities are kept in the dark and don't know how their lives compare with other parts of the country.

• Policy can't be evaluated and lessons learned.

• Everyone ends up spending lots of time and effort collecting their own data.

(PAT 18, 2000, p12)

With good data we can:

• diagnose the problem;

• develop strategies to tackle the causes rather than the symptoms;

• evaluate the outcomes;

• find out what works.

(PAT 18, 2000, p13)

The website for National Statistics (**www.neighbourhood.statistics.gov.uk**) was established and it collects data from a wide range of sources and presents it free of charge to anyone who wants to use it. The neighbourhood section allows you to find out lots of data for your area including comparisons with other areas. It is particularly useful to use the age cohort data to estimate the numbers of teenagers in the area (check you adjust for the age of the data). That is the good news. The bad news is that Local Area Agreements are still weak in their use of data and this is clear both in the reviews of Local Partnerships and the strong guidance about using data when developing the agreements.

I worked in a city where decisions were made by ward. This seems fair until you work in the area where many young people lived creating populations of 13,000 to 15,000 per ward; compared with the central wards where the old youth projects were with populations of 6,000 to 8,000 per ward. In 2004 the Office for National Statistics introduced 'Super Output Areas' (SOA). Using SOAs the country is divided into equal populations of about 1500 people. The website has digested most of the data into these units and the best community profiles are prepared using them.

Statistics are about morality. If you know the proportions of the population you can plan to meet their needs fairly. A democracy can debate and struggle to win freedom from want if you know the levels and location of want, ignorance, disease, squalor, and idleness (to adapt Beveridge, 1942). You can have a sensible conversation when you have the facts right. This is where we need to use the first definition of equality used in Chapter 3. Real equality can be shown in some numbers that are equal, and inequality is revealed by unequal numbers (such as the lower rates of women's pay). Building the distance from services into multiple deprivations allows us to begin to count how difficult it is for rural young people to take part in mainstream life.

Young people
Data taken from public sources will get you so far. It will indicate the significance of particular issues in your area. But it then needs to be connected to the real young people who live there. New projects, revised uses for facilities, evaluations of existing projects all require the managers and workers to go beyond the 'usual suspects' when they ask what is needed.

Young people need to have their needs met. I remain an enthusiast for the 'planning for real' approach of using big maps and models, prioritising systems, to which people can contribute: eyes down is better than eyeball to eyeball confrontations; moving cards around is better than endless talk (Gibson, 1998, p297). As many young people as possible should contribute, and if it is a long term plan, consider the young people who will be teenagers next.

Some of the best consultations are facilitated by trained young people who work with their peers. It takes time to prepare the young people who will lead the investigations but it has the benefit of building in 'youth proofing': it is likely to be clear and make sense to the young people.

Linking wider
We live in a democracy which is powered by conversations. One of the most striking developments of the last few years has been the range of people I have found myself in

conversation with in the name of youth work. For example: the Fire and Rescue Services in Cleveland, and Tyne and Wear devised experiential learning programmes as a way of reducing arson and nuisance calls; Cleveland Police have developed a marked respect for youth work and the law abiding character of most young people as a more effective way of reducing their crime figures rather than insisting on head-on confrontation policing. Certainly, not all that they do is youth work; but when we are defining need and planning there are comments to be heard from surprising partners. The Public Service Agreement (PSA) indicators can prove a short cut to finding out what they are likely to be.

Clarity of purpose

What are we here for? begins many good discussions. Local projects attracting voluntary enthusiasm and diverse pots of funding need to talk it through to stay together.

Marsha: *We need somewhere warm and safe for the kids.*

Jo: *I want them to make new friends and be happy in their lives.*

Al: *You ask me, but I'd like them to decide.*

Robin: *To widen their view of the world, we're pretty isolated here.*

ACTIVITY 7.2

- *Can you suggest a short phrase that answers the question for this group?*
- *How far do you think they have common ground?*
- *What might the risks be of conflict?*

Mission statements as sites of public ethics

A mission statement sums up the overall purpose of a project. It tells everyone why the organisation exists and the impact you want to have. It is expressed in broad terms and is supported by more detailed statements of aims, outcomes, and so on. You may not achieve your mission, but it indicates what you are striving for; the values you are expressing.

Statements that describe the purpose of the organisation are ethical statements. When you read the 'objects' of a charity, or the strategic purposes of a public service they state what that group of people have agreed to do, for the public benefit. The words define the activities, for the wider good.

Getting those words right at the start is a difficult task and is a joint task in ethical reasoning. Here are seven questions to start you off.

1 What is the range of good things we wish we could do? (Usually a long list.)

2 Who are the main beneficiaries?

3 Where are the limits of place?

4 What don't we want to do?

5 How do we want to work?

6 Why do we think that we should do something?

7 How do we summarise all this?

However, the start is not the only concern. Most of the time we work with established organisations. The written statements, particularly in constitutions and legislation, set the ethical tasks which we have to express. For people joining the organisation they need to decide if they want to sign up to these expressed values: this is particularly important if you are applying for a job – you would be a public face of the organisation. For managers and board members going back to these fundamental statements can give new insights when you are thinking through the new opportunities that you are being asked to take on. Are they what we are here for?

Missions tell people what you do; importantly, they remind you what you do. The best missions are constantly in your mind as a phrase that helps you prioritise work and time. They need to be short and clear and true.

ACTIVITY **7.3**

Here are nine statements by different organisations.

1 The National Trust was founded in 1895 'to promote the permanent preservation for the benefit of the nation of lands and tenements (including buildings) of beauty or historic interest'.

2 The British Canoe Union: Helping and inspiring people to go canoeing.

3 Southall Black Sisters was established in 1979 to meet the needs of black (Asian and African-Caribbean) women. 'Our aims are to highlight and challenge violence against women; empower them to gain more control over their lives; live without fear of violence; and assert their human rights to justice, equality and freedom'.

4 The mission of the youth service is to promote the development, well-being, rights, and participation of young people (age 4–25).

5 Calling a generation to dynamic faith, radical lifestyle, adventurous mission and a fight for justice.

6 Creating safe spaces for young people to explore personal, social, spiritual, and political choices.

7 Muslim Youthwork Foundation: responding to lives not events.

8 Girlguiding UK enables girls and young women to develop their potential and to make a difference to the world.

9 Scouting: join the adventure.

Task:

- *Identify which of these statements are strap lines evoking the character of the organisation and which are mission statements indicating the purpose of their activity.*

- *What are the strengths of each approach in telling others what you do?*

- *What are the strengths of each in telling members what you do?*

- *What do the mission statements tell you that the organisation is not going to do?*

Choosing between good things

Søren Kierkegaard wrote: *the purity of heart is to will one thing*. It is the task of managers and organisers to focus energy to make a difference in that area. This means making choices to create the space and time for the good thing to be done. Gordon Wakefield used to encourage his students to *murder your darlings*. There are all sorts of attractive or useful things but they must be dropped in favour of the good things (Aristotle again). More difficult is to pick between good things when there are so many. If you choose one, others will accuse you of being against two or three others. Choosing is a balance between personal decision and social discussion.

Let us explore this by looking at one of the oldest arenas of youth work: Christian youth work. The New Testament presents its readers with a wide range of sayings, stories and characters. Christians value 'calling' and 'mission' as ways they decide what to do.

Calling

Jesus called disciples to follow him and be his friends; calling is vocation (Latin). Read the following.

> As Jesus walked by the Sea of Galilee, he saw two brothers, Simon, who is called Peter, and Andrew his brother, casting a net into the lake – for they were fishermen. [19]And he said to them, 'Follow me, and I will make you fish for people.' [20]Immediately they left their nets and followed him. [21]As he went from there, he saw two other brothers, James son of Zebedee and his brother John, in the boat with their father Zebedee, mending their nets, and he called them. [22]Immediately they left the boat and their father, and followed him.
>
> (Matthew 4:18–22)

- Did these men know Jesus before he met them?

- How does the calling fit with their practical duties to their family and work?

- How does the lack of detail of the calling compare with the way you started youth work?

Calling is a recurrent theme in Bible texts. See for example: John 15:15, or I Corinthians 1:9.

Mission

Jesus sends his followers to go and do different, specific things; sending is mission (Latin). Read the following.

> Inherit the kingdom prepared for you from the foundation of the world; [35]for I was hungry and you gave me food, I was thirsty and you gave me something to drink, I was a stranger and you welcomed me, [36]I was naked and you gave me clothing, I was sick and you took care of me, I was in prison and you visited me. [37]Then the righteous will answer him, Lord, when was it that we saw you hungry and gave you food, or thirsty and gave you something to drink? [38]And when was it that we saw you a stranger and welcomed you, or naked and gave you clothing? [39]And when was it that we saw you sick or in prison and visited you? [40]And the king will answer them, Truly I tell you, just as you did it to one of the least of these who are members of my family, you did it to me.
>
> (from Matthew 25:32–46)

- What specific target groups are the readers expected to think about?

- What are they meant to do?

- How many of these groups are readers expected to respond to?

- Which public organisations express responses to this passage?

Bible texts are usually read in active groups who are wondering: how does that inform or direct the way I live my life? For many years English Christians would have the chance to read the whole of the Old Testament once a year and the New Testament twice a year: a wide variety of bible stories and themes. The challenge is to decide which of the good ideas to take forward.

ACTIVITY **7.4**

Cassie and the church council

Cassie is working for a church as a youth worker. The church council is supporting the work because their core purpose is expressed in quoting Matthew 28:19–20

> *Go therefore and make disciples of all nations, baptizing them in the name of the Father and of the Son and of the Holy Spirit, and teaching them to obey everything that I have commanded you. And remember, I am with you always, to the end of the age.*

They see the youth work as an opportunity to make the young people into disciples.

Cassie wonders if the young people might not have something to reveal to the adults in the church. She is confirmed in the idea that this might be a good idea by more words of Jesus which seem to put a particular focus on the special nature of vulnerable young people.

> *At that time the disciples came to Jesus and asked, 'Who is the greatest in the kingdom of heaven?' He called a child, whom he put among them, and said, 'Truly I*

ACTIVITY 7.4 *continued*

tell you, unless you change and become like children, you will never enter the kingdom of heaven. Whoever becomes humble like this child is the greatest in the kingdom of heaven. Whoever welcomes one such child in my name welcomes me. If any of you put a stumbling-block before one of these little ones who believe in me, it would be better for you if a great millstone were fastened around your neck and you were drowned in the depth of the sea.

(Matthew 18:1–6)

Task:

- *These texts are from the first century AD. What links can you see to the current legislation about children?*

- *What links would you make to safeguarding policy and legislation?*

- *What common ground is there between the two perspectives described?*

- *What are the differences in emphasis?*

- *What parallels can you draw between this contrast and the contrasts found in child safeguarding debates?*

Christian youth work is marked by a sheer range and variety of approaches and motivations.

It is important not to assume that you know what a particular project is up to.

Find out about their methods and target group by all means, but make sure that find out about their mission. Table 7.1 shows nine different motivations and purposes for youth work that can be found in churches.

ACTIVITY 7.5

Diamond nine: living with several concerns

Clearly, we need to choose. One effective way of doing this is to write each separate type of work on a separate card. In the case above, we now have a pack of nine cards. Ideally, a large group should work in pairs to agree the order of priority of the different good purposes. A diamond shape helps, with the most important at the top. Having worked in pairs form larger groups, fours and eights, and do the same task.

Parenting and intergenerational responsibility

Parents

Youth workers can react badly to a discussion about parents: parents can represent the limited scope of the young person's background and nurture; they can be the people who restrict young people's lives: an older generation, who are resisting changing times. On the

Table 7.1 Youth work in churches

Type of youth work	Purpose	Examples	Bible reference
1. Sunday school	To ensure baptised children become adults who know the faith	Robert Raikes started them; William Smith changed some into the Boys Brigade. *Children in the Way* (1988) challenged separation of age group and the educational methods.	Matthew 18:1ff, 2 Timothy 1:5.
2. Holy support groups	To make a space for young people to pray, reflect, worship and do things with peers.	Methodist Association of Youth Clubs, Church Pastoral Aid Society. They can be counter cultural, or seek to use youth culture to carry a deeper theme.	I Corinthians 13, Hebrews 4:11, 6:11, 12:1–13.
3. Evangelisation projects Service projects	To tell those who have never heard the Christian message of the meaning and purpose of life To act as a servant to the world	Mark Ashton *Christian Youth Work* (1986), Alpha courses. Homeless support, drug addiction.	Matthew 28:19–20 Matthew 20:26, Mark 10:45, John 13:4–16. Specfic focus: Matthew 25:32–46
4. Community development	To express the distinct contribution of Christians within wider society.	Faith in the city, unemployment campaigns, working in partnership in regeneration programmes.	Pastoral care: John 10:1–15. Yeast: Matthew 13:33, salt: Matthew 5:13. In the system: Genesis 41, Nehemiah, Daniel, Jeremiah, Isaiah.
5. Prayer and presence of God Practicing love	To make a place to be still and know God To offer unconditional love to all young people (not just Christians).	Taizé, Shepherd's Law. Open door youth work, Samaritans.	Exodus 3:1–6, Isaiah 6:1ff, Matthew 17:1ff Luke 22:40–46 Mark 10:45 1 Corinthians 13
6. Developing learning	To develop learning for life	Zaccheus Centre Birmingham, faith schools, training programmes.	Seeking abundant life for the learners: John 10:10 *the truth will make you free*. John 8:32
7. Rescue	To protect vulnerable children and young people	The Children's Society, Barnados.	Matthew 18:1–6.

other hand: parents are the people responsible for family life, the *fundamental group of society and the natural environment for the growth and well being of its members and particularly children.* (UN Convention, preamble 5). There are positive statements about intergenerational responsibility. Hillary Clinton used the Nigerian proverb: *It takes a village to raise a child.* President Obama (2009) included in his list of examples of faith and determination of American people: *a parent's willingness to nurture a child* and did do, as an act of courage, alongside hard decisions about shorter working hours in a recession, and rescuers responding to Katrina and 9/11. Parents can develop resilience in their children which can be effective in managing lives faced with complex challenges and risks (Hill *et al.*, 2007). But a single word or phrase needs to be checked and criticised for what it actually means.

> *Warm, authoritative, responsive and supportive parenting is usually crucial in building prospective resilience in children, as well as helping them deal with many specific adversities. Parents who have, or can develop, open, participative communication, problem-centred coping, confidence and flexibility, tend to manage stresses well and help the rest of their families to cope well. When parents are implicated in the problems (e.g. family violence, neglect), then it is particularly crucial for children to have access to additional or alternative helpers who fit with the children's needs, wishes and expectations.*

> (Hill *et al.*, 2007, p37)

If we take these insights and link them to youth work practice we can recognise the strengths and weaknesses. The descriptions of good parenting match processes we would expect in good youth workers. There are characteristics (warm, responsive, supportive, participative, problem centred, flexible) that will mean that parents might take or pick up their children, even when they are 17 or 18: it will be part of their curiosity and care for their child. Such parents can be good advocates for youth work in the wider community and they might take up voluntary roles to support the work.

The weaknesses are more difficult and youth workers are often disregarded in child welfare; making the role more frustrating. A young person may flee from home to the project, as a place where there are substitute parents. These youth workers may have the good parenting characteristics: 'Warm, authoritative, responsive and supportive' 'helping them deal with specific adversities', they have 'open, participative communication, problem-centred coping, confidence and flexibility'.

ACTIVITY 7.6

The relationship between parents and youth work creates difficult questions for the youth worker. Discuss each of the following in pairs and then in a larger group.

- *How do I manage the projection of a fantasy ideal parent and maintain boundaries?*

- *As the young person discloses aspects of life at home, what am I meant to do?*

- *As this young person has never learnt to behave well, their behaviour is time consuming and dominating groups: should I exclude them?*

- *How do I best manage their personal and social development?*

The value and benefits of intergenerational activity in communities in developing young people

Recent research into the development of young people has cast light on the impact of the benefits of different types of intergenerational activity.

Research review 1: Alternative parents; 'turnaround people'

When parental care is deficient, then children and young people who have formed at least one trusting and supportive relationship with an adult outside their family have been able to sustain progress despite exposure to risk, or to turn round highly problematic lifestyles (Werner and Smith, 1992, 2001).

Resilient children in troubled families often actively recruit and form special attachments with influential adults in their social environments (Walsh, 1998).

Supportive adults are frequently members of children's networks at school or in the community. But, for some, it is the more artificial allocation of a professional or mentor that proves vital (Gilligan, 1999a, 2001; Williams et al., 2001).

Benard (2002, pp 213–227) identifies three qualities that characterise individuals who help young people resist stress ('turnaround people').

1 A caring relationship.

2 High expectations.

3 Opportunities for contribution and participation.

In addition, American research has often highlighted membership of a faith community as a buffer against stress through both spiritual and social support (Werner, 1996).

(Hill et al., 2007, p14).

Research review 2: Leisure activities chosen by adolescents in 1986 and their relation on adult outcomes

Feinstein L, Bynner, J and Duckworth, K (2005) undertook a large study of the cohort of young people born in 1970, linking their activities as 16 year olds with their outcomes at age 30. They observed the following relations.

• Being healthy:

*   – being a smoker at age 30 was less likely with higher frequency of attendance at sports centres, uniformed youth clubs and church: frequency of uniformed youth club was negatively associated with single parenthood;*

> – *frequency of attendance at youth clubs increased the probability of being a smoker, and predicted single parenthood.*
>
> • *Staying safe:*
>
> – *sports and community centres also appeared to reduce the likelihood of living in temporary or social housing;*
>
> – *attendance at a youth club tended to predict adult temporary or social housing.*
>
> • *Enjoy and achieve:*
>
> – *sports and community centres, uniformed youth clubs (less so) and church-based activity enhanced the prospect of high achievement: plus: a steady rise in the size of the strength of the prediction as the qualification level increased;*
>
> – *youth club attendance showed the strongest relationships with poor educational outcomes.*
>
> • *Making a positive contribution:*
>
> – *racial intolerance appeared to be countered by church attendance at 16 and by being female;*
>
> – *voting was positively linked to being a member of a uniformed youth club and to church attendance;*
>
> – *memberships were most common among those 30 year olds who had attended, at 16, uniformed youth clubs, church leisure activities, and after-school lessons;*
>
> – *being an offender was positively predicted by youth club attendance. Serious offending was related only to youth club attendance.*
>
> • *Economic well-being:*
>
> – *low income was less likely among 30 year-olds who had attended sports and community centres, uniformed youth clubs and school-based leisure activities.*

What might this mean? Feinstein and colleagues have continued to work through their findings and present them in revised ways, in part because the findings are so unpalatable to youth workers. Perhaps the findings can be read in this context to highlight the value to young people of becoming adults in the supportive context of young people and adults. There is a greater tendency to find other adults in sports settings and churches, the volunteers in uniformed organisations operate in often better ratios than youth workers. The adults provide safe structures and expectations within which young people can make their choices (the Challenge, Counsel and Training expected by the Albemarle report).

Volunteers

Consider the voluntary motivation of many of those who give their time to young people's development and review the place of youth work within a wider range of public initiatives aimed at young people.

The youth service has always had a mix of volunteers offering opportunities to young people. It is very easy when faced with full time paid workers to concentrate on them when thinking about management. Volunteers change the experience for young people: they really are there because they choose to be, and because they want to be there for the sake of the young people.

Volunteers demonstrate that giving time and energy for the public good is worthwhile. They show that a democracy depends on people offering their insights and contribution. They express values beyond material reward. They match their own hope to be good people with the need of others to benefit from some unconditional positive regard.

This volunteering sits alongside some quite technical and precise professions that deal with young people, such as: teaching, nursing, policing. It creates a moral impetus to youth work that is more exploratory, hopeful, and variable than the established professions. It is a mix of good and bad and a reason for writing this book.

Social capital

The development of social capital (see Chapter 2) is another way of looking at the long term effects of youth work. Social capital can be a way of looking at the social development of young people. What sort of long term social development are we likely to achieve? Transformative youth work should make a difference to the young person's life chances. The report on the achievements of the youth service in 1986 (a time of recession and weak support of public services) suggests that it can fail to counter social exclusion.

Youth clubs can end up developing bonding social capital: reinforcing local ties, just focusing on association, avoiding counsel and challenge. Networking and national and international organisations can develop bridging social capital taking young people out of their setting and opening them to wider experiences.

Accountability

Giving an explanation about what we are up to is essential to good behaviour in youth work. We are using public resources; of time (including voluntary time) and money. We are working with young people who are vulnerable and whose parents trust us with their safety. Here we will review three main aspects of accountability: what are we accountable for? To whom do we give account (Vernis *et al.*, 2006, p98ff)? and by what means is this supported?

What are we accountable for?

Money

Even the smallest project handles some money and it must be clear how it benefits the young people and that it is not being used for the personal profit of someone else. Donors need to know that their money was received and the money was used for the purpose for which it was given. This reinforces the cycle of trust that builds up the credibility of an organisation and is true in the public and voluntary sectors. Publications of money coming in and money going out on youth work can be organised using clear financial accounting.

Management and suitability of staff

Time and money are valuable resources that need to be used in the most effective and efficient way. Saying how you have used the resources will need an explanation of the ways in which you plan and follow through their use. Work plans, project plans, budgets, setting milestones, devising Key Performance Indicators, and so on: these all make sure that the work is focused on benefiting the young people in the best possible ways.

The recruitment and education of staff are key sites of ethical action by projects. The suitability of the staff is specifically noted in the UN Convention Article 3. We discussed this in the previous chapter, but here I want to raise the issues of accountability for the way in which these tasks are carried out. Who works with a group of young people, and why they have been chosen are briefly matters of interest to job applicants at the interview stage. Nevertheless, we need to tell long term stakeholders: parents, partnership, and the other management committee members who were not involved in the process of selection. The issue of clear boundaries between the personal life and professional roles as youth workers (NYA principle 5) is reinforced by these processes. Interview panels need to declare conflicts of interest and we weaken the ethical status of youth work when family members and close friends appoint each other to jobs (see the Nolan principles).

Creating clear records of the process and developing those records to show how the staff have been supported in their learning to meet the requirements of the job will express, at management level, that same concern for the competence to do the job. Joint Negotiating Committees (JNC) of workers, educators, employers, and unions agree youth work learning, qualifications and pay and this is a final aspect of project accountability. It is part of good developmental youth work for workers and managers to be involved in the review, development, and management of the profession's qualifications: both at local NVQ level and in the University courses.

Impact on beneficiaries

Neighbourhood work, issue based work, and targeted work all have their specific beneficiaries. They are defined by age, location, interest, and sometimes other characteristics. It is true that we work with young people because they are young people (NOS, 2002, ii), but the current values statement accepts the specific nature of a lot of our work (NOS, 2008, p4). The YMCA was set up for young working men. Church of England parishes are geographically defined in their purpose and work. Charities have objects that define their purpose and scope. Local Authorities are there to serve a particular community. A project working with young homeless would be regarded as wasting money if it spent most of its time with young people who were not homeless.

Governance

Who the managers are is important. In the list of those who manage and in the consultation structures is expressed diversity, democracy, and shared accountability. These are themes we keep coming back to and this reflects the abiding role of youth work as an expression of the best aspects of our society.

The early days of youth work can get criticised for the dominance of 'philanthropists': they seem to undermine diversity. But Davies argues that the settlement movement and the emergent voluntary youth organisations pioneered *an important new expression of the true philanthropic spirit*. They *required their workers to engage directly and personally with young people, they set out to bind giver and receiver very closely together. Indeed these highly personalised interactions were to be the carriers of the moral education to be achieved* they *placed relationships at the heart of its practice and provision* (Davies, B, 1999, p11). The use of relationships as the key allows strong personal leadership to be moderated by the significance of a range of other people in the organisation: the impact of the powerful rich white man is not like his impact in commercial organisations: the relationships made by the women, the black workers, the young peer mentors create a corporate culture which is transformative of the young people, and perhaps wider society. What do you think of the Prince's Trust?

Who manages can define the influence being brought to bear. A project that gets public money from the local council will expect a local councillor or officer to join the management committee. Management committees who only represent one aspect of a population will probably be regarded as being excluding, or unrepresentative.

The structures of management and scrutiny allow projects to show and learn about democracy. The law certainly constrains the formal role that under 18s can exercise in governance. But the UN Convention on the Rights of the Child also states: *the child shall in particular be provided the opportunity to be heard in any judicial and administrative proceedings affecting the child* (UN, 1989, Article 12). This Article is committed to developing the competence of children in decision making, and this is a common feature of child welfare and Family Courts. Youth work is less personally acute. In a court or a Children's Trust a decision on one day can affect a child's life. In youth work we offer a setting where skills of judgement, representation and decision making can be developed gradually by young people. Effective youth work organisations have achieved this over many years and there are models to use. *The power democracy gives is exercised in the knowledge that one day it will be given back* (Clive James).

Strategic impact

The wider context of the work that is undertaken is also important. How do we focus our operations on the most relevant aspects of our mission, trying to contribute the most to society in our field (*Vernis et al.*, 2006, p99)? Looking up from the immediate and local allows us to match work to changing patterns of society, address Public Service Agreement targets, and give young people a sense of being part of the whole wide world.

To whom are we accountable?

Young people

The absolute focus on the benefit to the young person means that the first people we explain ourselves to are the young people. There should be no hidden agenda, vague and unthought-through plan, or manipulative activity. Clear planning and engagement with young people means that we will, inevitably, be subject to legitimate questioning and asked for explanations. Much of this will be spoken, but there will be written documents. Projects may agree styles and standards to improve the way these are written. Plain English crystal mark may define really effective communication. Some projects help 'youth proof' publicity and public plans to get to the heart of what affects the young people. Others consider the insights of literacy specialists and dyslexia research by using particular type faces, font sizes, and paper colours. Most projects are concerned with their presence on the internet: how can the site express clearly the main priorities, and allow participation without becoming a place where bullying or misinformation starts. As we stated before the choice of the young people about what they do is at the heart of youth work and this needs to be made a reality by transparency and a clear flow of information.

Parents

Projects that look after young people need to have regular, clear lines of communication with the families who are their main source of love and support (UN Convention Article 5 and preamble 5 and 6).

Article 5: *States Parties shall respect the responsibilities, rights, and duties of parents or, where applicable, the members of the extended family or community as provided for by local custom, legal guardians or other persons legally responsible for the child, to provide, in a manner consistent with the evolving capacities of the child, appropriate direction and guidance in the exercise by the child of the rights recognized in the present Convention.*

Programmes need to tell parents what activities are going to be undertaken and at what times and how particular requirements will be met for expertise and safety. If we don't do this, how informed can the parental consent be? Parents are, above all, the people who need to see the paperwork that relates to the risk assessment for the activities their young people will take part in. Regular flows of information and replies giving details of diet or medical requirements and, above all, permission to take part build the trust needed by youth workers.

The parents should also be the first contact when there is a problem for the young person. This is fairly obvious if you are away with a young person and have a list of contact details. What happens if you are doing detached youth work and find a vulnerable drunk girl in the bushes? Good youth workers use a vehicle, to provide a safe place; and a phone call to the parent to pick them up. Multi-agency meetings might ask: what powers are you using? No power at all; just persuasion and the building of trust. The girl is safer (from risks of: sexual abuse, violent attack, or choking on vomit), and better able to be cared for by their family (than being arrested, or made subject of a cause for concern report). For the young person they are safe and sound, and for the parent they are part of a society that is also trying to do the best for their teenager.

All this seems normal and reasonable. It is significant that the communication with parents is a weakness that has been highlighted in Inquiries into the behaviour of other professionals. Here are two examples.

1   The 1987 Inquiry into child abuse in Cleveland. Recommendation 3 states: *parents should be given the same courtesy as the family of any other referred child. . . Parents should be informed and where appropriate consulted. . .* (Butler-Sloss, E, 1987, p246).

2   The 1999 Stephen Lawrence Inquiry. It reviewed the way the parents of the young man was treated and concluded: *From the first contact. . . Mr and Mrs Lawrence were treated with insensitivity and lack of sympathy. . . Mr and Mrs Lawrence were not dealt with or treated as they should have been. They were patronised. They were never given information . . . to which they were entitled.*

(Macpherson, 1999, p318)

In both inquiries, the professional had chosen to use some characteristic of the young people and their parents to close down proper communication to the parent: suspicion of abuse, or a racist conviction that the young black man and his family didn't deserve the same service. Youth workers can develop their own fantasies and prejudices: the young people choose, the young person is growing up and becoming independent from their family; therefore the parent does not need to be kept fully in the loop. Certainly, young people choose and they are growing into adult responsibility for themselves; but they also have relationships to negotiate with their parents, and part of our work is to share the care of the vulnerable young person with the parent.

Management meetings and line managers
Regular meetings allow the rapidly changing work to be explained and explored. Sticking to the time and place allows the establishment of a commitment to attend. Sudden cancellation breaks the trust and weakens the team work.

Line management for most youth workers oscillates between the polarities of supervision and performance management. The wrestling with nuance and lack of formal power makes the supervisory and reflective approach of the independent professional attractive. It is also part of the tradition of youth work (Tash, 1967). But, it must be clear from the extent of the accountabilities that independence of view will not work for a profession that is so woven into wider structures of family, democratic administration, local community, and the law. There comes a point at which the job description and the project plan which have been developed by extensive debate and agreement need to be defended. Public time and money ends up being protected by the performance management conversations in local projects. Managers who focus only on the worker, privilege the worker over the other stakeholders in the youth work.

Monitoring bodies
The main principle here is truth telling. Different projects have different bodies to report to, but accurate reports are essential to build support and justify the privileged position that you have to spend public time and money working with young people. Spaces are created and resources allocated for this specific purpose and the formal relations of accountability are there to provide a final check on the validity of the activities that have been undertaken under the umbrella of this formal arrangement. Local Authority projects will need to explain

how their work is progressing. Ideally such reports will be scrutinised by elected representatives and not just officers. They may be subject to public questioning and this is reasonable. Finally they will also be subject to inspection in various forms, for example, by Ofsted or the National Audit Office. The voluntary and community sector report to the Charity Commission and Companies House. These reports are also made public for all to see and can be followed up where aspects of reports are not satisfactory. Funders also expect regular reports on progress and reports must connect with the original basis of the funding agreement. Care in going back to the original plan is certainly necessary but real truth springs from the regular work being aligned to the agreed plan.

Wider community

Youth work is a privileged activity.

- It makes little direct contribution to the economy.

- It is expensive to do well (excellent, well maintained buildings, programme costs to open opportunity to all and experienced, qualified staff all cost money).

- It creates special settings for young people who are often annoying to wider society and a cause for concern to their parents.

- It is given legal protection by specific statute (Education and Inspections Act, 2006), and by charity laws.

With privilege comes responsibility and it is up to us to explain what we do, how we do it, and why this is a good thing. The best projects have excellent websites, persist in publishing reports, ensure they have regular press releases, and organise open activities and displays. Building trust builds support.

The most contested polarity is that between the bad behaviour of young people (Anti Social Behaviour) and the bad behaviour of adults towards young people (Child Protection from abuse). Give a clear account without dismissing either end of these debates.

ACTIVITY 7.7

Play schemes and community capacity

The context: the estate is mainly local authority properties and there are plenty of young families, often headed by women on their own. Transport is expensive and the ring road acts as a moat closing off the outside world. There is a community centre used for parties.

A youth worker in the voluntary sector encouraged parents of young people to meet in the spring because of the stories of boredom from young people stuck on the estate throughout the summer holidays. A group forms who agree to train up and staff a weekly activity throughout the school holidays. The training happens around Easter and there are applications made for funding. The estate is leafleted and the programme is oversubscribed: each young person pays a daily subscription and there is space for 56. The programme includes an introductory session with icebreakers, ground rules, and explanations of the programme; there are several bus trips out to the countryside and seaside with activities, it all ends with a games day and celebration in the centre. The success of the programme means it happens each year.

Local authority youth work on the estate has been at a low ebb. After two years of the voluntary scheme the council announces new sessions twice a week in the summer holidays: 10 am–12 noon and 2 pm–4 pm, in the community centre, staffed with sessional workers from the estate. The take up is poor: a maximum of 12 young people, and typically 6. The motivation to plan is weak because there are often different young people.

Questions
- *What are the strengths of each provision?*

- *What are the weaknesses of each provision?*

- *How was capacity built?*

- *What values do you see expressed in the two pieces of youth work?*

- *How do the provisions compare as value for money?*

- *What would you suggest to the youth service?*

Consistency

Ensuring consistency is a common theme in management. Consistency is challenged by arguing that it works less well in dealing with people than it does in the production of things. I do not agree with this and we will look at a five areas which reinforce the need to be consistent in youth work design and management.

Focus on learning, personal and social development of young people

Article 1 UN Convention on the Rights of the Child:

For the purposes of the present Convention, a child means every human being below the age of 18 years unless under the law applicable to the child, majority is attained earlier.

Each young person needs the same quality of focus. Each activity needs to be clearly developmental and planned. For managers this means more than young people ticking a box somehow labelled 'accredited outcome.' Managers need to be reviewing learning plans; educationally designed activities that create processes for the personal and social development of young people. Anything less must fall short of the requirements of the 2006 Act.

One great benefit of focusing on learning (by the young people) is that it increases the interest in learning (within the whole organisation) and their ability to adapt. Organisations increase their reliability by learning: they get feedback from users and staff, they organise events to develop new insights, they develop a culture where reporting is seen as a good thing and near misses are analysed (Munro, 2008, p128ff).

Addressing discrimination

Article 2 UN Convention on the Rights of the Child:

* *States Parties shall respect and ensure the rights set forth in the present Convention to each child within their jurisdiction without discrimination of any kind, irrespective of the child's or his or her parent's or legal guardian's race, colour, sex, language, religion, political or other opinion, national, ethnic or social origin, property, disability, birth or other status.*

* *States Parties shall take all appropriate measures to ensure that the child is protected against all forms of discrimination or punishment on the basis of the status, activities, expressed opinions, or beliefs of the child's parents, legal guardians, or family members*

Explicit focus on tackling discrimination is important because we know how systematic failure can be expressed in a number of combined behaviours. The Stephen Lawrence Inquiry, for example, identified *a combination of professional incompetence, institutional racism and failure of leadership in connection with Stephen Lawrence's racist murder* (Macpherson, 1999, p317ff):

* Officers failed to show basic First Aid skills in which they were meant to have been trained and retrained.

* Officers failed to document the murder inquiry properly from the earliest stage.

* The family were not treated properly.

* Individual managers did not intervene, made poor decisions, and allowed things to drift.

* Follow up investigations were poorly planned and executed: *the team was simply going through the motions* (1999, p319).

* Illegal behaviour and the bad behaviours associated with it in the form of racism and institutional racism had become an accepted part of the work culture (1999, p321).

* There is a particular need to re-establish trust between minority ethnic communities and the police (1999, p323).

* Demonstrating fairness is not enough to achieve this trust *it must be accompanied by a vigorous pursuit of openness and accountability. . .[senior managers] should be vicariously responsible for the actions of their officers* (1999).

* Where there are public services that operate with public consent, improving them to achieve equal satisfaction across all ethnic groups is an activity that involves genuine partnership that includes all sections of the community (1999, p325–7).

The Stephen Lawrence Inquiry focused on the police and not the youth service; addressed a murder and not informal learning. But the themes identified above can be used as a managerial audit of the youth service. More explicitly, the Inquiry recommended that the National Curriculum used in schools, and the management of schools should prevent and address racism (1999, p334–5). Since the Lawrence Inquiry, the Cantle Report (2001) and Education and Inspections Act 2006 have reinforced the need for youth work to include consistent provision that addresses the needs of BME young people and monitors performance.

ACTIVITY 7.8

Using the Lawrence Inquiry themes to reflect on practice.

In your youth work setting.

- *How do you test the use of basic First Aid skills in which workers have been trained and retrained?*

- *How do staff document the social development programmes to address racism, both in terms of their design and impact?*

- *How does the project monitor the engagement with families to check consistency?*

- *What opportunities are made for individual managers to intervene, make decisions, and stopping things from drifting?*

- *What areas of work seem poorly planned and executed, the team simply going through the motions, just ticking boxes? How might this be remedied?*

- *Are there ways in which racism and institutional racism are accepted parts of the work culture? What can be done to address this?*

- *Is there trust between minority ethnic communities and the project? How can trust be built?*

- *How does the project vigorously pursue openness and accountability? What are the regular systems and activities that engage with the BME communities in the area? How are the managers vicariously responsible for the actions of the workers?*

- *Is there equal satisfaction across all ethnic groups about the delivery of the youth service? Is there genuine partnership that includes all sections of the community? What mechanisms achieve this?*

Ensure that risks are managed

Consistent organisations manage risk so that potential hazards do not cause harm. Reviewing who or what might be harmed we can list: the young people, the youth workers, and the organisation that serves the young people. This will also be the order of priority of managing risk.

Article 3 UN Convention on the Rights of the Child:

- *In all actions concerning children, whether undertaken by public or private social welfare institutions, courts of law, administrative authorities or legislative bodies, the best interests of the child shall be a primary consideration.*

- *States Parties undertake to ensure the child such protection and care as is necessary for his or her well-being, taking into account the rights and duties of his or her parents, legal guardians, or other individuals legally responsible for him or her, and, to this end, shall take all appropriate legislative and administrative measures.*

- *States Parties shall ensure that the institutions, services and facilities responsible for the care or protection of children shall conform with the standards established by competent authorities, particularly in the areas of safety, health, in the number and suitability of their staff, as well as competent supervision.*

Youth workers do not start from the position (like the medical profession) that the people we work with will bleed, suffer some discomfort or pain, have their dignity infringed, and even cease to be conscious; as a consequence of our intervention. When youth workers define risk they do so in the expectation (like air traffic controllers) that they will achieve a continuous run of incident free interventions.

However, we also start from the position that being an adolescent is a risky business. Young people are developing adult needs but do not yet have the skills and knowledge to manage them. Young people want to meet with others but do not have their own place. Young people are more likely to suffer violence and crime. Young people may experience the risks of poverty more acutely. Youth work starts from the presupposition that the harm that might come from any of these risks can be avoided or reduced by skilful youth work. In some sense it continues to be a 'rescue' service (Spence, 2001). Before we judge other risks we need to ask: will a failure to act increase the risks in the lives of the young people? Addressing these fundamental risks, there will be accompanying risks that need in their turn to be managed. That balance of risk management and the offering of activities is expressed in NYA ethical principle 3. Putting the benefit to the young person at the heart of the service while looking outward, building on the strengths of an open and participative culture is the way in which the 1991 report encouraged youth workers to move forward (Coopers, Lybrand and Deloitte, 1991, p606).

C H A P T E R   R E V I E W

In this chapter we have emphasised the underpinning design and management of youth work as sites for ethical decision and practice. Long term and short term statements and behaviours show the focus and open accountability of youth projects and their participants to wider stakeholders. Youth work looks back home to the family the young person comes from and to the wider society that sets high standards of practice.

Excellent management that works well with local communities is the best way to achieve many of the themes discussed here.

Chambers, R (2002) *Participatory workshops.* London: Earthscan. Good tools for finding out and deciding can be found in this book.

Reason, J, Hayes, R and Forbes, D (2000) *Voluntary, but not amateur: a guide to the law for voluntary organisations and community groups,* sixth edition. London: London Voluntary Service Council. Good advice and detailed development of management, constitutions and projects can be found from this continually updated book.

REFERENCES

Ashton, M (1986) *Christian youth work.* London: Kingsway.

Benard, B (2002). Turnaround people and places: moving from risk to resilience, in Saleebey, D (ed.), *The strengths perspective in social work practice,* 3rd edn. Boston: Allyn Bacon.

Beveridge, Sir W (1942) *Social insurance and allied services.* London: HMSO.

Butler-Sloss, E (1987) *Report of the inquiry into child abuse in Cleveland 1987.* London: HMSO.

Church of England Board of Education (1988) *Children in the way.* London: National Society (Church of England) for Promoting Religious Education.

Davies, N (1999) *The isles.* Basingstoke: Macmillan.

Evers, A and Wintersberger, H (1990) *Shifts in the welfare mix: their impact on work, social services and welfare policies.* Vienna: European Centre for Social Welfare Policy and Research.

Feinstein, L, Bynner, J and Duckworth, K (2005) *Leisure contexts in adolescence and their effects on adult outcomes.* London: Centre for Research on the Wider Benefits of Learning.

Gibbon, FP (1934) *William Smith of the Boys Brigade.* London: Collins.

Gibson, T (1998) *The power in our hands.* Charlbury: Jon Carpenter.

Gilligan, R (1999a) Working with social networks: key resources in helping children at risk, in Hill, M. (ed.) *Effective ways of working with children and families.* London: Jessica Kingsley.

Gilligan, R (2000) Promoting resilience in children in foster care, in Kelly, G.and Gilligan, R. (eds) *Issues in foster care: policy, practice and research.* London: Jessica Kingsley.

Gilligan, R (2001) *Promoting resilience: a resource guide on working with children in the care system.* London: BAAF.

Hill, M, Stafford, A, Seaman, P, Ross, N and Daniel, B (2007) *Parenting and resilience.* York: Joseph Rowntree Foundation.

Kierkegaard, S (1952) *The purity of heart is to will one thing.* London: Hodder.

Munro, E (2008) *Effective child protection.* London: Sage.

Nolan Report (1994) *First report of the committee on standards in public life.* London: TSO.

NOS (2002) *National Occupational standards for youth work.* Grantham: PAULO.

Obama, B (2009) Presidential inaugural speech, 20 January 2009.

PAT 12 (2000) *Report of policy action team 18: young people.* London: Stationery Office.

PAT 18 (2000) *Report of policy action team 18: better information*. London: Stationery Office.

Petit-Zeman, S (2006) *How to be an even better chair*. Harlow: Pearson.

Tash, J (1967) *Supervision in youth work*. London: National Council for Social Service.

United Nations (1989) *Convention for the rights of the child* (**www.unicef.org/crc/**).

Vernis, A, Iglesias, M, Sanz, B and Saz-Carranza, A (2006) *Nonprofit organisations*. Basingstoke: Palgrave.

Wakefield, G (1983) *A Dictionary of Christian spirituality*. London: SCM.

Werner, E (1996) Vulnerable but invincible: high risk children from birth to adulthood. *European Child and Adolescent Psychiatry*, 5: 47–51.

Werner, E and Smith, R (1987) *Vulnerable but invincible: a longitudinal study of resilient children and youth*. New York: Adams, Bannister and Cox.

Werner, E and Smith, R (1992) *Overcoming the odds.* Ithaca NY: Cornell University Press.

Werner, E and Smith, R (2001) *Journeys for childhood to midlife: risk, resilience and recovery.* Ithaca NY: Cornell University Press.

Williams, N.R, Lindsey, E.W, Kurtz, P.D and Jarvis, S (2001) From trauma to resilience: lessons from former runaway and homeless youth. *Journal of Youth Studies*, 4: 233–53.

WEBSITES

Bible references can found swiftly using **www.bible.oremus.org/**

Charity Commission **www.charity-commission.gov.uk/**

Companies House **www.companieshouse.gov.uk/**

Federation of Community Development Learning **www.fcdl.org.uk/**

Neighbourhood Initiatives Foundation **http://www.nif.co.uk/**

Chapter 8

Ethics and research in youth work

CHAPTER OBJECTIVES

Good youth work is well informed and uses accurate information in all that it does. Youth workers can be the makers and advocates of knowledge about young people and youth work practice. The development of arguments and information has a considerable impact on the resources deployed to affect young people's lives. Thoughtful and careful research and publication beyond reports of successful ideas is part of creating youth work as a profession, able to articulate (literally 'profess') what it stands for. This chapter will explore the ethics of researching young people, as part of youth work, and the benefits of such research for young people and for youth work.

Links to the National and Professional Occupational Standards for Youth Work 2008

Principle activity area	Examples of Units
4 Develop youth work strategy and practice	1.1.7, 1.3.3, 2.3.2, 3.2.1, 4.1.1, 4.2.1 , 4.2.3, 4.2.7 ,4.3.2, 4.4.1, 5.3.2

ACTIVITY 8.1

Setting up home

One afternoon I drove a former academic to visit a small group of young people and their youth worker. He was in the House of Lords and effective at raising social issues. The house was a hard-to-let local authority property secured by the youth workers to house homeless young people who had been living in the open. We were made a cup of tea and sat on the floor of the almost unfurnished, but warm, house while the young people talked. They described how they had ended up homeless because parents couldn't afford to keep them and pay the poll tax. They were pleased to be warm and dry. They did not see how they would get work. They were not studying and had no plan to do so. Clearly they were pleased to have somewhere their mates could come to. In the car home the peer remarked that it was hard to use the material as the press would have a field day.

Discuss: do you agree with the peer, and why?

Good research: doing it right

Finding out is a result of curiosity or knowing that you don't know. Research starts there but is not just a private quest: the public setting of the work place or a public qualification means that what we find out needs to relate to other people. Research can be defined as *a class of activities designed to develop or contribute to generalizable knowledge* (World Health Organisation).

Research in general

Research ethics are a particular place where the differences between ethical approaches are reproduced. Here we will break them into four different types, and divide them into two broad groups: teleological and deontological. Teleology focuses on the result: the end point of whatever has been planned. In research the results are usually the end point. Deontology takes the focus off the people, the 'beings'; and centres on the basic moral law: what must be done.

Teleological: ethical egoist

Nietzsche proposed: *egoism belongs to the essence of the noble soul. . . other beings will by nature have to be subordinate to a being 'like us' and will have to sacrifice themselves* (Nietzsche, 2002, p162). Following this line, the researcher is the person who needs to get a good result. They need to gather the right data to finish their study and get the marks for the assignment or the publication credit. Good research benefits the researcher in the first instance.

Teleological: utilitarian

This approach (associated with Jeremy Bentham and John Stuart Mill) is often summed up as achieving 'the greatest happiness for the greatest number' of people. The public as a whole needs a good result. It might even be possible to calculate how many people benefit from the research and the ubiquity and comprehensiveness of the results would justify the work.

Deontological: duty

Kant argued that *there is only a single categorical imperative: act only in accordance with that maxim through which you can at the same time will that it become a universal law* (Kant, 1997, p31). In your actions you are focused on their effect on other people. You ask: *What if everyone did that?* It helps researchers to turn the research question round to themselves and see how they react to being asked. Is this a way in which I should behave in this setting? What is my duty to the research subjects?

Deontological: rights

This approach focuses on rights that apply to everyone. Rawls summed this up in two principles. First: *each person is to have an equal right to the most extensive scheme of equal basic liberties compatible with a similar scheme of liberties for others* (Rawls, 1971, p60). Second: *Social and economic inequalities are to be arranged so that (a) they are to be of the greatest benefit to the least-advantaged members of society (the difference principle)*

(b) offices and positions must be open to everyone under conditions of fair equality of opportunity (Rawls, 1971, p302).

Usefully, we have lists of rights such as the US constitutional documents or the UN Convention on the rights of the child. Researchers can therefore include rights of children and young people in their proposals for research. For example: they can protect the rights of children to their identity (Article 8), privacy, honour and reputation (Article 16), and the role of the parent in the life of the child (Article 18).

ACTIVITY 8.2

Difficult decisions for researchers

Here are debates that arise for researchers. As you read them decide which ethical approach is challenged by each one.

- *Why should you research us? You'll become famous and we'll get labelled.*

- *We are a minority and our rights are being ignored because you are focusing on the general trend of the population.*

- *I have specialist knowledge and understanding that has been paid for by publicly funded education and research grants. Only I am likely to study this important subject and we need to have a better understanding.*

- *Protecting the subjects of your research means that they do not benefit from redistributive changes that might follow the research.*

Researching young people's lives

Youth workers are less concerned with research in general. We want ethical guidance on researching young people's lives. Nietzsche might make the job easy for us: just get on with it and produce the report. Mill would encourage us to look at the whole community and consider the different stakeholders. Don't assume that the interests of the older people should be neglected. The characteristic emphasis on process by youth workers means that there are significant attitudes towards the young people as subjects, and behaviours by the researchers and young people that are explicit in the agreed codes. The NYA code principle 1 refers to the respect that we are to have for young people and that this will have practical implications for avoiding exploitation and discrimination; and to manage confidentiality well. These are common themes with good practice in much social science research. The National Occupational Standards go further in describing the way youth work operates.

> *It recognises the young person as a partner in a learning process, complementing formal education, promoting their access to learning opportunities which enable them to fulfil their potential.*

> (NOS, 2008, p4)

These research principles match well with related areas of research.

> *The British Educational Research Association (BERA)believes that all educational research should be conducted within an ethic of respect for persons, respect for knowledge, respect for democratic values, and respect for the quality of educational research.*

This is spelled out in responsibility for participants in the research.

- They have the right to be informed about why the research is being done and how it will be made public.

- Participants need to give informed consent to take part. (We discussed competence earlier and the same issue applies here with the effect that a school may give consent for research to happen, and may also seek parental consent for the decision.)

- Care should be given in interviewing children, because of their vulnerability.

- Honesty and openness should characterise the relationship between the researcher, institution and participants. (So, researchers shall behave with integrity, there must not be hidden agendas or questions seeking secret results.)

- Participants can withdraw from the study at any time.

- Researchers should be aware of cultural, religious, gendered and other differences in the planning, conducting and reporting of research.

(BERA, 1992)

ACTIVITY 8.3

Planning research

You are undertaking a community study. The main purpose is to develop your skills in finding out and reporting what life is like for young people in an area. Complete the following tasks.

- *Write a short statement explaining to possible participants why the study is being done and who will find out the results.*

- *For the study you are going to talk to some 12 year olds at a school, 17 year olds at college, and some adults in a community centre. Write a consent plan for each of the three groups: who will need to agree?*

- *From the Local Authority and National Statistics data for the area you can see that there are lots of issues to find out about. You will need to focus on three. Which of the following will be the most suitable to ask all three groups about?*

  - *distance from the city centre;*

  - *exercise and fitness;*

  - *GCSE results;*

ACTIVITY 8.3 continued

- *literacy;*

- *numeracy;*

- *public transport;*

- *sexually transmitted diseases;*

- *worklessness;*

- *teenage pregnancy;*

- *youth work buildings.*

Epistemology for youth work

Research can make knowledge. It is a process that shares some common ground with other disciplines. We can divide the processes of knowing that make the final knowledge into three.

Knowing about young people

Knowing about young people is the obvious starting point. Commonly available data may be shared with other researchers. Health professionals might have an interest in the physical changes that young people go through and the behaviours they adopt. It is useful to step back from the social construction of young people to consider the value of adolescence as an evolutionary response to developing large brains (Bainbridge, 2009). Sociologists look at the social settings, agency, and power relations experienced by young people. Parts of this knowledge will be quite objective and factual; other parts will be constructions of how we can understand young people. We can call this cluster 'youth studies.'

Knowing young people

Youth workers have a privileged understanding of young people because they work with them each day. This means that they are reflective about their own interactions with those young people and this gives a particular character to their overall understanding. Other educators might look at the tendencies young people have to learn and change in social settings and the interactions that help or hinder. So too youth workers might use action research to develop their practice and explore who the young people are.

Being known by young people

Finally, the centrality of the relationship for youth workers means that being known by young people has an effect on our knowledge. You may be known as unreliable, or as a close friend. Either extreme will affect what young people will tell you. Greater trust may lead to greater disclosure, which in turn means a greater risk for the young person and greater care on your part. Young people will also occupy themselves by critically challenging ideas you have, not least, about them.

Benefits of research for young people

Youth workers can benefit young people by undertaking and publishing effective research. Research can identify who needs time and money, and can analyse good ways of working that need to be supported.

ACTIVITY 8.4

Read the NYA principle 4 and the UN articles 27 and 30 and answer the questions that follow.

NYA principle 4
Contribute towards the promotion of social justice for young people and in society generally

Practice principles would include:

* *promoting just and fair behaviour, and challenging discriminatory actions and attitudes on the part of young people, colleagues and others;*

* *encouraging young people to respect and value difference and diversity, particularly in the context of a multi-cultural society;*

* *drawing attention to unjust policies and practices and actively seeking to change them;*

* *promoting the participation of all young people, and particularly those who have traditionally been discriminated against, in youth work, in public structures and in society generally; and*

* *encouraging young people and others to work together collectively on issues of common concern.*

UN Article 27
* *States Parties recognise the right of every child to a standard of living adequate for the child's physical, mental, spiritual, moral and social development.*

* *The parent(s) or others responsible for the child have the primary responsibility to secure, within their abilities and financial capacities, the conditions of living necessary for the child's development.*

* *States Parties, in accordance with national conditions and within their means, shall take appropriate measures to assist parents and others responsible for the child to implement this right and shall in case of need provide material assistance and support programmes, particularly with regard to nutrition, clothing and housing.*

* *States Parties shall take all appropriate measures to secure the recovery of maintenance for the child from the parents or other persons having financial responsibility for the child, both within the State Party and from abroad. In particular, where the person having financial responsibility for the child lives in a State different from that of the child, States Parties shall promote the accession to international agreements or the conclusion of such agreements, as well as the making of other appropriate arrangements.*

ACTIVITY *8.4* *continued*

UN Article 30

In those states in which ethnic, religious or linguistic minorities or persons of indigenous origin exist, a child belonging to such a minority or who is indigenous shall not be denied the right, in community with other members of his or her group, to enjoy his or her own culture, to profess and practise his or her own religion, or to use his or her own language.

Questions

• *What knowledge about young people makes work with them particularly difficult?*

• *What are the most unhelpful constructions of young people?*

• *How does the work you are involved in reflect an inclusive approach to young people?*

• *What other questions have been raised for you by reading these passages? What knowledge about young people makes work with them particularly difficult?*

Muslim youth work in Britain

Muslim youth work is an area where there are ambiguous and underdeveloped ideas. This provides fertile ground for thinking through wider questions of evidence based practice in youth work. In this section you are going to read some data and consider ways in which you might develop understanding of the subject and develop youth work.

Demographics

ACTIVITY *8.5*

The population profile of Muslims in Britain has a particular character. Read the following facts taken from the 2001 census and answer the questions that follow.

National Population

• *The 2001 British population total was 57,103,927.*

• *There were 11,460,801 young people between 0 and 16.*

• *20.07 per cent of the whole population are between 0 and 16.*

• *45 per cent of the whole population are under 34.*

• *1 in 5 are under 16.*

• *1 in 6 over 65.*

Muslims

• *3 per cent of the British population are Muslims.*

• *There is a Muslim population of 1,588,890.*

ACTIVITY 8.5 *continued*

- *The 2001 census reported 535,853 Muslims between 0 and 16.*

- *33.72 per cent of the Muslim population are between 0 and 16.*

- *71 per cent of the Muslim population are under 34.*

- *1 in 3 are under 16.*

- *1 in 25 over 65.*

Questions
- *In terms of size, what is the significance of the numbers of young people in the British Muslim population?*

- *How does this compare with the numbers of young people in the wider British population?*

- *How do the proportions of people over 65 compare?*

- *What might the numbers mean in terms of priorities for youth work?*

Interpreting, constructing and imagining Muslim young people

ACTIVITY 8.6

British Muslim young people have highly contested identities. Here are 10 influences on the making of knowledge in this area. Either: work in a group with different people speaking for the impact of a paragraph on public understanding; or: write individual assessments of each paragraph answering these questions.

- *How does this affect the truth of statements about young Muslims?*

- *How does this affect the reliability of arguments about young Muslims?*

- *What areas of new learning does this suggest?*

  1 *The Parekh report (2000) advocates re-imagining who the British are: People in Britain have many differences, but they inhabit the same space and share the same future. All have a role in the collective project of fashioning Britain as an outward looking, generous inclusive society.*

  2 *Demonisation of Muslims by media: 91 per cent of articles monitored over a week in national newspapers about Muslims were negative (Guardian 2007).*

  3 *Dr Salman Sayyid describes the British population conceiving of British Muslims as immigrants, despite birth and education in the UK. Immigrants become citizens, in this mind set by being absorbed into the British way of life. Absorption, meaning being assimilated rather than assimilating, is seen as the only engine of transformation, where*

continued movement from one generation to another, particularly in terms of success or failure becomes a significant . . . predictor of future social behaviour (*Sayyid, in Ali et al., 2007, p22*).

4 *14 February 1989 Imam Khomeini issued a fatwa against Salman Rushdie, author of the Satanic verses. The argument lined up western liberals defending freedom of expression against Muslims who see removing the detoxification of western culture from their lives as an essential part of their identity (Khan, S, in Ali et al., 2007, p182).*

5 *The policy of Preventing Violent Extremism (2007) has a high public profile and drives much of the activity at local and national government level in response to the needs of British Muslims.*

6 *The Cantle Report (Guardian, 2001) into the riots in Bradford, Oldham, and Burnley criticised local authorities for encouraging separated, polarised, culturally uniform communities to develop by a combination of housing and other public policies. It leads to the policy of Community Cohesion.*

7 *Fifty-two people die in suicide bombings in London on 7 July 2005. The bombers were Hasib Hussain, Mohammad Sidique Khan, Germaine Lindsay, and Shehzad Tanweer: three of the men were from the Beeston in Leeds, Lindsay was from Aylesbury.*

8 *Ordinary lives where persistent racism expressed itself in violence, criminal damage and was not followed through the criminal justice system, so that it is invisible.*

9 *Claire Alexander comments:* there has been little scholarly work done on contemporary Asian youth identities, so . . . characterisations remain primarily at the level of speculation rather than fact. . . my own work on *The Asian Gang* (2000) suggests constructions reflect more a series of common sense assumptions than any discernable empirical reality. (*Alexander,C, in Ali et al., 2007, p267*)

10 *In 2006 the creation of the Muslim Youthwork Foundation:* responding to lives not events. *It aims to:*

• *support and promote Muslim youth work to initiate and develop sustainable opportunities for young Muslim people to reach their full potential;*

• *provide a platform that connects the voices of youth workers and young people to policy and government;*

• *generate and connect critical thinking to policy and practice;*

• *provide support and expertise to organisations and bodies seeking to develop youth work with Muslim young people or wishing to develop Muslim approaches to this work.*

The benefits of research for youth work

'Evidence based practice' is a phrase that is used a lot, but often without much understanding. What does it mean and what is it criticising?

In medical settings evidence based practice seeks to use the most effective treatments and avoid pointless or less reliable interventions. Arguments about the impact of this on health services are seen in the reluctance of patients to accept statistical evidence of reliability, and tests demonstrating the validity of a regime. Perhaps we might see 'alternative medicine' as a reaction to this rigour.

In social settings like youth work the debate is difficult. How far can we demonstrate real effects in complex human systems, especially with modest interventions like youth work? There is debate in youth work about the limits of 'positivist' research and value of 'interpretive' paradigms. But we do improve our practice (usually using a form of action research) and can make links between other projects and our own. Pawson and Tilley (1997) proposed a good way forward in epistemology and methods by asking researchers to match up configurations of context, method, and outcomes so that the transfers of understanding and practice can be made. Denying that we can learn anything seems not only pessimistic but also guaranteed to leave decisions to be made on the basis of some other principle rather than evidence, need or fairness.

RESEARCH SUMMARY

Policy Action Team 12: young people

Policy Action Team (PAT) 12 was a project conducted by the Social Exclusion Unit and the findings were published in 2000. Clearly, the research was about the state of young people's lives during the 1990s; but the themes identified there can provide youth workers with lines of inquiry, and the results can also set a benchmark for research that we might undertake. All youth workers should read the report. Here are the key points.

- *A large minority of young people experience a range of acute problems. On many indicators these are worse than other comparable nations.*

- *The risk of ending up homeless, unemployed or with poor educational qualifications is not a lottery (PAT12, 2000, p8). It is more likely among those who are poor, disengaged by education, over-subject to peer pressure, bullying, and inadequately served by the public sector. It is particularly acute among the BME young people.*

- *Government services have been weak.*

- *There have been gaps in services, particularly to prevent problems arising. This reflects bad design of services, and a failure to respond to new problems.*

- *Money has not gone to the right place. It should increase to meet the needs of the most deprived areas, but this has not always happened.*

- *Policy makers have failed to consult young people resulting in poor services and alienation.*

- *Policies and services have been fragmented: working in isolation or at cross purposes.*

- *We need to use what we know to improve services for young people.*

Youth work needs and allocating resources

Commissioning and planning youth services in Beckendale.

Accurate up to date information is essential for youth services to deliver a service that is meeting young people's needs in a way that is fair. Beckendale has received the latest population data for the wards in the authority. Regeneration (in the old docks area of Headland and Quay) and new housing (in the outlying estates of Gooners and Intake) has changed the patterns of where people live quite a lot in the last decade.

Ward population data

Ward/Ages	0–9	10–19	20–39	40–59	60–80	Ward Total
Market	25	134	4236	3312	2112	9819
Beck	1232	2311	4887	1233	423	10086
Dale	2214	2219	4321	335	355	9444
Colliery	237	134	2111	3344	4327	10153
Foundry	218	158	322	3311	5317	9326
Headland	1225	1225	2552	2543	2503	10048
Quay	1329	1235	3578	1546	2483	10171
Central	75	336	4236	3312	2112	10071
Kate	1785	1885	2652	2443	1463	10228
Allert	2567	2326	4448	435	365	10141
Epple	1325	1355	2699	2143	2528	10050
Gooners	298	268	352	3311	5322	9551
Intake	2317	2222	4440	365	366	9710
Laming	2511	2822	4115	310	397	10155

Questions

• Which are the six wards where you would want to secure neighbourhood youth provision?

• Central and Market are the wards that attract young people from across the authority at weekends. What are your arguments for and against youth provision in these wards?

• Which wards are likely to be places where older residents complain about the young people? What sort of provision might help, and why?

Three valuable activities in research

I have covered ground that many general discussions of research ethics might also address. But for youth workers the discussion is a very practical daily issue that has direct consequences for the young people we work with. Research is often done quietly, on your own, in preparation for a meeting, or a funding proposal. Sometimes a team is brought together to work on a strategic approach to youth work (like the review of services in Beckendale), or to undertake specific research projects like the government's Policy Action Team 12 (PAT12, 2000), or funded by the Joseph Rowntree Foundation or another major charity. Teams allow a checking of ethical approach to a greater extent than when you work on your own: you have to discuss what themes you can draw out and the reasons and arguments for choosing them. As we end this chapter let's highlight three themes that are virtues that researchers pursue in their work.

Telling the truth

The first virtue of a researcher is telling the truth. We set out to find out what is the case, and we try to overcome the mistakes that can be widely held. A mistake at the beginning of an argument, that is widely discussed, can be difficult to dislodge from the public mind and can have a cumulative effect in the development of arguments. As David Hume described the development of arguments by good talkers: *one mistake is the necessary parent of another, while he pushes on his consequences, and is not deterred from embracing any conclusion, by its unusual appearance, or its contradiction to popular opinion* (Hume, 1748, p2). In telling the truth we need to go back to the beginning of a series of facts and check that they are all still true and that the argument lines up as it used to. We are not dealing with refined elements of matter that we can expect to respond and react in fairly predictable ways, but in complex human systems that are subject to considerable variation and changed influence over time.

Telling the truth seems a reasonable thing to do until you build in the extent to which the facts and interpretations about young people's lives are contested in society. The characterisation by society of young people as bad and wrong was captured memorably in Stanley Cohen's *Folk devils and moral panics* (1972). The cover of the third edition (2002) uses a photograph not of the original mods and rockers but of young French Muslims in the banlieue of Paris being controlled by riot police: the application to incidents in Peckham or Bradford works too. Small incidents are taken in a polarised society to contain symbolic truths about the section of society from which the population is alienated. Big incidents create memories which become the lenses through which current reality is seen.

To make truths in this setting takes more than scrupulous attention to accuracy by the researcher – although that is an essential prerequisite if youth work is to have any credibility. Truths about young people are social truths and they need to be developed in social settings. We are good at getting young people to participate in the development of their services and typically this involves young people, officers and elected members from an authority. The risk here is that there are premises of the argument that were decided before the meetings happen. For instance: because the popular view of adults is that young people are marginal, therefore the county budget will build and improve roads rather make sure that schools are adequately furnished or staffed to ensure excellent education for young people.

One of the few benefits of the Northern Irish 'troubles' is that it produced useful insights into resolving conflict. Researched understandings of young people tend to be detailed, nuanced, and complex. Silence allows easy answers, simple stereotyping, and justifiable aggressive acts. Colum Sands' song summed up the approach: *whatever you say, say nothing* (Fitzduff, 1988, p155). To break down the stereotypes and prejudging it was a good idea to increasingly create groups and spaces where things could be talked through. Corrymeela brought together

Protestant and Catholics; and some clergy became vital in creating dialogue between Sinn Fein, and the Dublin government, and Unionism (Fitzduff, 2002, p33). Groups were formed to talk through Parades (2002, p65), Police complaints (2002, p82), and now there is power sharing at Assembly level with all the difficulties that come with it. It is particularly useful to see the way in which understanding and action were developed in different ways at different levels. I find that it helps navigate where to take a particular campaign to improve understanding by looking at an assessment of levels of power and methods to be used in the Northern Irish process (Lederach, 1995 cited in Fitzduff, 2002, p176).

Table 8.1 Levels of power and methods to be used in the Northern Irish process

Levels of power	Methods
Level 1 Main power brokers	Mediation
Governments	Problem reframing
Politicians	Political agreements
Paramilitaries	Ceasefires
Security Leaders	Military containment
Level 2 Power holders	
Statutory bodies	Equality work
Security forces	Security interface
Public bodies	Anti-intimidation work
Churches	Interchurch work
Educational institutions	Cooperative work
Trade Unions	Anti-sectarian work
Cultural institutions	Cultural pluralism
Businesses	Economic development
Level 3 Community power	
Community groups	Joint issues work
Women's groups	Contact work
Reconciliation groups	Rights work
Interface Workers	Challenge to paramilitarism
Prisoners	Political discussion

ACTIVITY 8.8

Questions

- *What are the equivalent groups at the three levels who have effective power in deciding the truth about young people?*

- *What activities will help the development of truth telling at each level?*

- *The conviction that things can get better was matched by a willingness to address issues in the short, medium and long term. What do you do to encourage the truth about young people to be known in the short, medium and long term?*

Fairness

Telling the truth is strongly linked to fairness. True statements reflect a fair resource devoted to creating them; a fair attitude in constructing them allows sufficient listening to the facts, and fairness in placing them alongside other statements. These are personal behaviours and yet they are to be found in organisations where professionals use their individual power to either advance or undermine a good understanding of young people. By pinpricks of unfairness the balloon of truth is deflated so that it will not rise sufficiently to improve young people's chances. So, you will hear it said: *young people were invited to be stakeholders* and *we all know what that means* and *we consulted in the area with the highest rate of arson*. In the processes described: the invitation did not ensure effective engagement or facilitation, the new insight was hidden by a reference to an existing interpretation, and the voices were distorted by the emotional response to disorder. With a little less care the truths about young people can become rumours, slander, or libel.

Truth telling also links to fairness in the consequences of what has been found out. Accurate facts and interpretations allow resources of time and effort to be focused on the people and places where there is the most need. They allow transformational interventions and plausible configurations of methods and anticipated outcomes.

Creativity

Kerry Young concludes her book, *The Art of Youth Work* (1999, p122), with a quotation from Spinoza *all things excellent are difficult as they are rare* and her own comment that practice is not just based on addressing *current social problems and political priorities, but on a commitment to developing the truly lifelong goals of rational judgement and authentic human existence*. Testing ideas for youth work begins in our own creativity and some of the response to what we choose to do will be found in the future, unknown character of young people. We don't know what the authentic responses to future situations will be and no matter how much we accept the accountability of rationality and seek the development of good habits of life there needs to be scope too for creativity.

Creativity is needed in responding to what is found out about young people's lives because it often seems that nothing works. Programmes, interventions, targeted areas seem to show little change, some negative results. What do we do with these uncomfortable results? One response is to deny the research and pick holes in it. A better response is to look at what seems to cause the trouble, and to see if there are any hints about what to do instead. Feinstein's research (2005) is pretty miserable reading for mainstream youth workers, but the more robust ones have reviewed their practice to see how they might ensure better personal and social development for young people and perhaps include some inter-generational activities. In short: they have found spurs to be creative.

The cost of doing nothing is evident in the alienation of people who are excluded from a thriving society. The cost of doing nothing is also seen when an activity has a good result. The unlocking of the conversations between young women and their GP as a result of the Gillick court cases, and the more imaginative opening hours and locations of contraceptive services have made it easier for the young people to want the child they give birth to.

Miklós Erhardt had an exhibition at Secession in 2008 based on the experience of taking an abandoned shop in the peripheral Havanna estate in Budapest. He was given lots of suggestions about what to do with the shop: *'a pawn shop; a 'money laundry' advertised as such; a drug shop dealing in a wide range of stuff from simple synthetic glues up to heroin; cheap alcohol; a photo studio combined with a dating agency, advice for local people having legal problems with the local government, a public toilet, a grassroots youth club, a microwave salon where food could be heated'* (Erhardt, 2008, p24). But, with blistering honesty, he reflects on the emptiness of how it actually turned out: *Having a shop in a place where there's virtually no business, results in you becoming a strange object to contemplate and in you contemplating yourself.* By trying to integrate in the local setting he actually experienced greater distance between himself and his own activity. He therefore sought to complete the work by talking himself out of the situation. He produced a video. *Besides the video, another development is that the shop in 50/9 Havanna Street is waiting for the next tenant clean and tidy* (2008, p35). What can we make of this? *A belief in the possibilities of productive failure* (2008, p42).

Like Miklós Erhardt, Irving Welsh used creativity to make vivid the reality of socially chaotic and contradictory lives lived next to the mainstream. Many youth workers knew about the widespread impact of heroin in the 1990s but it may have been more widely heard as a result of the famous lines: *Choose us. Choose life. Choose mortgage payments; choose washing machines, choose cars; choose sitting on a couch watching mind numbing and spirit crushing game shows. . . Well, ah chose not to choose life* (Welsh, 1993, p187ff). It may not just be neat tables and graphs that convey the facts effectively.

C H A P T E R   R E V I E W

Research is characteristic of graduates and postgraduates: they usually write a dissertation exploring and developing a particular subject. For youth work courses this is a great opportunity to develop and share new insights. Excellent work can be edited for publication in journals. But research is essential for youth work to assert young people's space in society. New generations of young people mean that the data is often out of date. If we are going to do good youth work in the right places we need to tell the truth to make sure they get a fair deal.

FURTHER READING

There are many good books to support independent research projects.

I like Cohen *et al.* (2007) for the sheer range of methods explained and discussed.

Students find manuals on how to do your dissertation a big help, but they seem to vary on which particular one makes the most sense to them.

I like Pawson and Tilley (1997) a great deal. Their *History of evaluation in 28½ pages* is excellent for its clarity and wit. I particularly like the practical suggestions that they make and have seen them applied by project researchers and managers with great success.

Alexander, C, in Ali, N, Kalra, VS, and Sayyid, S (eds) (2006) *A post colonial people: south Asians in Britain*. London: Hurst and Company.

Ali, N, Kalra, VS, and Sayyid, S (eds) (2006) *A post colonial people: south Asians in Britain*. London: Hurst and Company.

Bainbridge, D (2009) *Teenagers: a natural history*. London: Portobello.

Cohen, S (1972/2002) *Folk devils and moral panics*. London: Routledge.

Cohen, L, Mannion, L and Morrison, K (2007) *Research methods in education*. Abingdon: Routledge.

Department for Communities and Local Government (2007) *Preventing violent extremism pathfinder fund*. London: Department for Communities and Local Government (**www.communities.gov.uk**).

Erhardt, M (2008) *Havanna – intervention in public space.* Vienna: Secession.

Feinstein, L, Bynner, J and Duckworth, K (2005) *Leisure contexts in adolescence and their effects on adult outcomes*. London: Centre for Research on the Wider Benefits of Learning.

Fitzduff, M (1988) *Community conflict skills*. Cookstown: Community Conflict Skills Project.

Fitzduff, M (2002) *Beyond violence*. Tokyo: United Nations University Press.

Guardian (2001) 11 December Key points of the Cantle report.

Guardian (2007) 14 November. *Report on Media Study showing demonisation of Muslims.*

Hume, D (1748) *An enquiry concerning human understanding*. London: A Millar.

Kant, I (1997) *Groundwork of the metaphysics of morals*. Cambridge: Cambridge University Press.

Khan, S, in Ali, N, Kalra, VS, and Sayyid, S (eds) (2006) *A post colonial people: south Asians in Britain*. London: Hurst and Company.

Nietzsche, F (2002) Beyond good and evil. Cambridge: Cambridge University Press

NOS (2002) *National occupational standards for youth work*. Grantham: PAULO.

Parekh, B (2000) The future of multi ethnic Britain. London: Runnymede

Pawson, R and Tilley, N (1997) *Realistic evaluation*. London: Sage.

PAT 12 (2000) Report of policy action team 18: *young people*. London: Stationery Office.

Sayyid, S, in Ali, N, Kalra, VS, and Sayyid, S (eds) (2006) *A post colonial people: south Asians in Britain*. London: Hurst and Company.

Welsh, I (1993) *Trainspotting*. London: Minerva.

Young, K (1999) *The art of youth work*. Lyme Regis: Russell House Publishing.

Chapter 9
Setting ethical priorities and explaining them

In the old days youth workers were called youth leaders. The idea was that they would give young people moral leadership. We might start using the term again, but apply it to showing leadership among other adults in the ways we might behave towards young people. Such leadership needs the ability to think through contradictions and build on values. This chapter will make a few suggestions about how this might be done.

Leadership can be a lonely task (Julia Middleton, in Petit-Zeman, 2006: it is timely to remind you that this is not a minor matter only of interest to those of us who are youth workers.

> *All too rarely do I hear people asking just what it is that we have done to make so many children's hearts so hard, or what collectively we might do to right their moral compass – what values we must live by. Instead I see us doing what we've always done – pretending these children are somehow not our own.*
>
> (Obama, 2007, p438)

But this is someone who doesn't just have unreal expectations of virtues that have no place in difficult settings; this is the reflection of someone who had watched the attitudes of those who work in the most deprived communities.

> *Some were there only for the paycheck; others sincerely wanted to help. But whatever their motives, they would all at some point confess a common weariness, a weariness that was bone deep. They had lost whatever confidence they might once have had in their ability to reverse the deterioration that they saw all around them. With that loss of confidence came a loss in the capacity for outrage. The idea of responsibility – their own, and that of others – slowly eroded, replaced with gallows humour and low expectations.*
>
> (Obama, 2007, p230)

Ethical argument has the purpose of helping us make the right choices, but it also can have the effect of renewing our confidence and helping us articulate our justifiable outrage at the way young people's lives are being determined. In this chapter we will look at two ways of using the ethical codes, we will consider how to use the virtues we have been discussing, and we will conclude with a discussion of youth work as an educational activity.

NYA code

Prioritising is not being unethical

One of the most disappointing results of studying ethics on university based youth work courses is the conviction among professional youth workers that the work they do is unethical. I have taught a Master's level programme for six years and we attract mature workers who undertook Diploma level qualifications a decade ago, and it is surprising to hear them condemn their own cutting edge practice in this way.

My suspicion is that the discovery that one ethical principle is less significant is taken as a judgement against the goodness of the work which may be achieving other important principles. We will explore this in a couple of ways. Firstly: I will make some remarks about the philosophy of this. Secondly: we will work through two case studies where we prioritise using the NYA code.

Kierkegaard's view was that *within [our] cultural, historical and philosophical situation there are nothing but relativities, arbitrary choices, and various kinds of immediacy. None of these situations provides the absolute reference. It is only by the absolute relation to the absolute that these relativities find their place* (Smith, in Macquarrie, 1967, p188). Youth workers will recognise the relativity of their work: always less important than others who make policy, have bigger resources of buildings, money or legal power. You will also recognise the almost arbitrary nature of decisions negotiated with young people, managers and parents: they seem to turn out less logical and structured than we might have hoped. You will also recognise the immediacy: you have to react quickly, responding without the chance to talk to partners or bosses who are all off duty. For me, the well crafted ethical code begins to express (as a whole) a more stable absolute, which I refer to. Making the connection to at least part of that code is crucial. As Kierkegaard wrote *the purity of heart is to will one thing.*

ACTIVITY **9.1**

NYA ethical code cards

For the case studies that follow you will need to make a set of eight cards. Each card will have written on it one of the NYA ethical principles. Ideally, the words need to be large enough to be easily read in a group. I encourage you to make a good job of this so that you can reuse the cards when you are working. I have a set made by sticking address labels on some spare playing cards.

Duke of Edinburgh award example

Consider the following situation:

A group of young people (15 years old) you are working with approach you. They have heard about the Duke of Edinburgh (D of E) scheme and want to do it. They are particularly attracted to the expedition: the idea of camping up in the Scottish borders and walking with rucksacks with their friends seems brilliant.

You know the young people a little and can think of the possible glitches. None of them has camped before and in fact some of them have rarely been out of the town where you work. You wonder too about their stamina, both in terms of physical endurance and in the long term commitment needed for D of E.

You also know that the youth service has become more cautious about outdoor activities. In the past it was a big thing but now it is regarded as not very inclusive (attracting boys rather than girls, white rather than black, and excluding young people with impairments). One of the senior managers has developed risk assessment forms that put most people off and the view is generally held that D of E is run in the schools rather than the youth service.

But you can also think of the benefits for the young people. It would be a project that would develop each of them personally. Their social development both as a group and in relation to wider society would be excellent (just think of the social capital the award would give each of them). Besides, there are good places to develop some of the skills nearby before they go to the Borders. Finally: they'd have something to tell their grandchildren.

With these conflicting thoughts buzzing round in your head you wonder what to do for the best. You buy yourself some time by suggesting that the young people read up about the detail on the website. While they do that you get out the pack of eight ethics cards and lay them out on the table in front of you. You move them around, trying to decide which the most important principle is here: that one goes at the top, like the point of a diamond. Next to it you put a couple more that are less important, but support the first one. Gradually you use up all the cards in about five layers. The last one, at the bottom, is least significant.

ACTIVITY **9.2**

Try arranging the ethics cards and see what order you put them in. When you are happy with the order explain it to someone else and see if they agree with you. You can always move a card if they suggest something to improve it.

Here's the argument we came up with when we discussed it.

Top of the list was principle 1: treat young people with respect. This is their idea, their enthusiasm and in the end they will have to have the energy and skills to do it. Young people are capable of developing to complete D of E awards: and very impressive they are too. Surely, there are enough good things in what we know about these young people to justify these high hopes. And if there aren't, well it's a pretty depressing thought. It is a bit like the telegram sent by the absent father at the start of Swallows and Amazons: *Better drowned than duffers if not duffers wont drown*. Somewhere in there he was delighted by the people they were growing up to be.

Next, side by side, were numbers 2 and 4: young people making choices, and social justice. The whole process will give them lots of chances to choose so they can practice decision making and get better at it. The consequences are practical so that will be a good way to learn. Besides, if they don't get the chance to do it with us they can always choose to do it somewhere else, maybe by themselves – which may be worse. The social justice theme is important here too: these young people don't get easy support to go and do this sort of thing. They go to an outdoor centre for a week once at school, but their parent isn't going to buy them a tent or take them youth hostelling. It shouldn't just be the middle classes who use the national parks and long distance footpaths: the Kinder Scout trespass of 1932 wanted access for all. So what that the Local Authority has worries about inclusion: let's make sure it's a good mixed group.

Next row down, were two drivers for the underpinning work that would be needed for it to go ahead, principles 6 and 7: being accountable, and developing the skills to do the job. The accountability has a lot of themes: young people, parents, service managers, the D of E scheme itself, and the worker. The young people will be developing skills and this will be a careful process so that they build up what they need. But it will be a development for the worker too: they've not done it before and will need to find out what is needed and who can help. Both accountability and skills development will need to start and be maintained throughout the project.

Lower down: the welfare and safety of young people, and keeping good boundaries (principles 3 and 5). These need to be done but they must be the servants of the main principles that are driving the project.

Finally, principle 8: working for conditions where ethical principles are discussed and evaluated. This is something that will be done, especially in the accountability part of the project. But placing it down the bottom of the priority list reminds us that arguing about how the youth service is run may be more important to the workers and mangers than it is to the young people. Given the choice between dreaming of the heather beneath their feet and being stuck in a committee with the head of service which do you think the young people would rather do?

ACTIVITY **9.3**

Discuss the arguments made here. Do you agree? How would you improve the proposal?

Drinking and detached youth work

Consider the following situation:

A detached youth work project works in an area of small flats and maisonettes near the middle of town. There are lots of young people on the streets because it is often too crowded in their homes to meet their friends. At the weekends, particularly, groups of young people are holding informal parties with drink and music in the public spaces of street corners, bus stops, and so on. The local paper has been running stories of young people's drunkenness and this has raised the temperature of the conversations. Local councillors say they don't want council money encouraging drinking. Youth service managers think that it looks like condoning illegal behaviour. Residents want the youth workers to deal with the kids. The workers themselves find young people they know coming up to them when they've had a few, because they are known and they worry about the safety of the young people.

Discuss: what is the biggest problem facing the youth workers?

The youth workers talk through their options. Using the NYA code they begin to prioritise the ethical principles. They split the cards into three divisions.

The first division has three cards that address the problem they have with the adults.

The second division has three cards that address working with the young people.

The last two cards are less important.

The first group has principle 6 at the top: be accountable. Their work is in the public eye. There is a risk that they will end up being told not to work with some of the young people. This would be stupid rule as it would probably be broken. Supporting the principle are principles 8 and 5: organise an ethical debate and keep sensible boundaries. These three principles need to be brought alive in this setting otherwise the workers will not be allowed to express any of the other principles that apply more directly to work with the young people.

The workers prepare for a meeting. They decide to get the different stakeholders together. They prepare with a group of young people who are willing to talk about what it is like finding somewhere to meet and something to do in their spare time. They also invite some of the residents from the area. They invite the local councillors and their own managers to come and listen. They set a very tight agenda of areas of discussion to give the young people the chance to discuss their concerns and hear the reactions of the adults. They plan a follow up meeting for the managers, councillors, and the workers to talk through what they have heard. Finally they will have a follow up public meeting to see what might be done in practice.

Their hope is that the meeting will allow them to advocate the ethical principles 1, 4 and 3 which are the centre of their concern for the work with young people. Hearing the young people's point of view (when sober) may increase the likelihood that they will be treated with respect (1). It might be a bit clearer that the overcrowding, in most of the accommodation, raises issues about social justice for the local authority in terms of giving the young people the chance to meet (4). Finally the welfare and safety of the young people might be taken a little more seriously when faces and names can be put to the threat they apparently pose (3).

There are two ethical principles that are less important here and will not form a major part of the discussion. The first is the choices that young people make (2). Arguing for this is more difficult as young people are losing their status as competent, credible adults by being drunk. The second is the competence of the workers to do the job (7). They judge that they can make a sensible proposal of how to continue to develop their detached work and manage the sequence of meetings.

ACTIVITY 9.5

Discuss the arguments made here. Do you agree? How would you improve their proposed plan?

UN convention on the rights of the child

Youth workers can use the UN Convention as a way of developing practice. It certainly underpins the developing legislation and policy in the UK, but it is also possible to take the Articles directly into the practice context. Sometimes a government agency or local people will assert that this Article should not apply in this situation. Perhaps the role of the professional youth worker is to continue to stand on the side of the young people and assert the rights which have been given to all young people. Here are two case studies to help you consider the idea in more depth.

CASE STUDY

Woody the refugee

The dockworkers were full of the story of the boy on the timber ship. They'd been unloading hardwoods from the East and he'd been found unconscious with an empty water container and a handful of possessions. But there was a pulse and he'd been lifted out, an ambulance called, and he was recovering in hospital. It had been quite a morning and they thought they should go and see how he was getting on. One of them had a twelve year old who looked about the right size and was going to pick up a few clothes for the lad who had been dressed for the tropics; he also thought of the youth worker his children knew and gave them a ring: can you come with us?

A strange request, but the youth worker went along. After all, the boy was entitled to some rights and it was not clear who would stand up for him: there'd no doubt be issues about why he was there and how he should be treated. Certainly he had not been in his 'patch' but he was now and the worker should go and see to make the first three rights in the convention come alive.

1 Every young person under 18 has rights under the Convention.

2 The Convention applies to all young people, no matter what their background or origin.

3 All those who work for young people should work for the best for each young person.

At the hospital the boy is conscious and being looked after; he should recover. The dockers explain who they are and the staff are happy for the visitors to see him; they explain about the youth worker and they are taken on one side to talk through what is going on. The youth worker offers to help and the hospital staff are pleased to have it.

The worker reviews what needs to be done.

- *Article 6: young people have the right to life. The hospital has done this.*

- *Article 7: the young person should have some sort of identity document, surely he is registered somewhere? This proves more difficult. There are bits of newspaper that suggest that the boy is from Indonesia but no passport or identity card. It is possible he was never registered: only 43 per cent of rural children are, and 69 per cent in the towns.*

(UNICEF 2006:134)

Hospital managers suggest that DNA tests or dental tests might indicate age and origin, and it would be easy to do while he's not fully conscious. The youth worker says this seems a bit excessive: surely they'd ask permission from other patients?

- *Article 12 gives the boy the right to say what happens to him. So, they would do better to wait until he's more conscious and can talk.*

- *Article 16 gives the boy the right to privacy. It would be invading his privacy without consent to do those tests, no matter how good an idea it might seem.*

The youth worker agrees to go and do some research to make sure there are others to help. They contact the Mission to Seafarers who are used to dealing with language problems and the rights of (adults) from other countries who find themselves in the UK. They talk to their line managers in Children's Services, explaining what has happened and asking for the right people to help. They also think through the longer term: perhaps they will need the rights in Articles 15, 20, 22, 28 and 29?

Discuss

- *What are the strengths of the way the youth worker behaved?*

- *What are the risks that they face?*

- *When asked about boundaries, the worker commented that it was part of their professional status in their community to have responded when the dockers asked. List the possible reasons they might have for this view.*

- *Do you agree with the Articles chosen? Which would you not use? Are there others you might follow up?*

Virtues: attitudes to others

So far in this book we have reviewed a series of 'virtues' or habits that youth workers might exhibit to be typical of their profession. As MacIntyre (1985) argues more generally, social accountability is more important for youth workers than being regarded as the great individuals of Nietzsche's writing (1985, p257). If we follow MacIntyre's argument further we would seek to cultivate these habits represented by the virtues. This may result in some restraint in other areas of our lives: *commitment to sustaining the kind of community in which the virtues can flourish may be incompatible with the devotion which a particular practice requires* (MacIntyre 1985, p201). So it may be that getting young people to join your cause or using them to illustrate your ideology or belief will not do, and you'll have to choose between the youth work and the other concern.

List of virtues seen among youth workers

Here is a list of 18 virtues that we have seen elsewhere in the book. In each case the virtue is elaborated a little.

1 Friendship – benefit the friend rather than your own pleasure or profit.

2 Integrity – approach life as a whole, and be honest and consistent.

3 Care – respond to meet the other person's vulnerability and need.

4 Accountability – explain to others what you are doing.

5 Association – spend time with other people.

6 Equality – give each person the same respect and authority.

7 Listening – pay attention to others.

8 Overcome discrimination – address unfairness and prejudice.

9 Fairness and justice – stand up for the right judgements.

10 Put young people first – before the organisation, or the worker.

11 Value diversity – discover the range of human lives.

12 Don't abuse power – no cheap tricks, remember your privileges.

13 Young people make (informed, consenting) choices – let them really choose.

14 Education – the best way of achieving change, using thought, and application.

15 Safety – cause no harm.

16 Improve groups – groups need care, like individuals, and have power too.

17 Make it easier for people to take part – we're all learning and meeting new people can be part of that.

18 Tell the truth and check the facts – this one brings several of the others together.

ACTIVITY 9.7

Picture this

Take a virtue from the summary list of 18 and create a poster that names and illustrates the virtue. A group might work together to express all 18 visually.

Deciding what to do

Postmodernism

In the old days it seemed easy enough for youth workers in training. Students were encouraged to identify their own values and then to realign them with the values of youth work. We used to be pretty vague about those values: there were no codes, no occupational standards.

Some might say we live in 'postmodern' times: the big narrative that could be relied upon to give a common purpose for a community would mean that there is not as clear as it was. There were of course several narratives: Christianity, Marxism, Islam, liberalism, free market capitalism, and so on. Christianity became less powerful as the common story in the UK as the twentieth century developed, but has a different role in other parts of the world (Davie, 2002) so that it can now be seen as deviant or alternative. Political Marxism suffered a major setback in the late 1980s and early 1990s such that it will need substantial work to overcome its fall and bad reputation for mass murder. Davies (1996, p1329) gives an estimate of 54 million killed in the USSR, excluding war dead, 1917–1953. Islam is currently wrestling with the rejection of modernity or an accommodation that will allow wider conversations. You can continue the list, and will no doubt include the doubts about the banking systems found in 2007 and 2008 that continue as I write. We don't have easy common ground.

One of the responses to the end of neatly organised modernism was to doubt the real possibility of any ethics. Postmodernism can be characterised as:

> *laid back and playful,*
> > *it distrusts logic and rationality,*
> > > *. . . it refuses to judge.*

> *Pick 'n' mix avoids the difficult and disquieting*
> > *Babble replaces discourse and dialogue*
> > > *Everything is good for a laugh*
> > > > *. . . opinion passes for truth.*

(CBF, 1996, p9)

But this won't do for youth workers. We have to give an account of ourselves. Of all professions, we seem to work with short term projects and the account we give to get the next tranche of money has to explain our processes and the effect of what we have done. If we are giving an account, explaining, and arguing then we must find some common language so that others will know what to expect from youth workers.

We have to make judgements too. Young people's well-being is too important to joke about. Appalling treatment of young people can't be bluffed through; better behaviour needs to be developed. Abuse and death of young people at the hands of adults, workers, and other young people is not an ambiguous matter: we should be working to stop it.

Using ethicists

I have referred to eight ethicists. They are a great and stimulating read.

1 Aristotle (2000): the man who started the systematic writing about ethics – still helping students distinguish why we do things.

2 Aquinas (1920): who wove together Aristotle and Augustine in a world beating pattern of dialectic – still a challenge to Christians.

3 Kant (1997): trying to express as logically as possible the good behaviour of his Lutheran society – still getting us to check our logic.

4 Hume (1739–40): who gets us to prove our points a bit better.

5 Nietzsche (2002): who reminds me of how powerful my sense of my own importance can be, and leaves me wondering how to avoid going with his argument.

6 Bonhoeffer (1995): who disturbs the neat patterns: *the knowledge of good and evil seems to be the task of all ethics. The first task of Christian ethics is to invalidate this knowledge* (1995, p21).

7 Rawls (1971): the great advocate of rights; read this to think thoroughly about rights.

8 MacIntyre (1985): who wishes to remove the enlightenment, everything since Hume and Kant, and depend on the virtues. His dissection of the players is masterly, but I find it hard to forget those other voices.

These philosophers challenge our expressions, order our contrasting arguments, and help us judge the sources of our views and values. Good students of youth work will be curious about how to improve in these areas: developing better use of words, practicing criticality that can be used in other contexts. Read the originals as well as the secondary literature they are in good translations and are often clearer than their interpreters.

But philosophers use a great number of abstract nouns and verbs. I have tried to use real incidents; some named as historic practice, some hidden to save embarrassment. Actual incidents where choices have been made seem to be some of the best ways of growing ethical skills. One advantage of the NOS is that students have to give examples of how they have done their work embedding values of youth work. Choices are what we are faced with and so we need to think about how they worked out for good or bad. In part, this approach reflects the English tradition of Common Law where cases were compared to ensure the development of consistent judgement, rather than first setting out a code. It also reflects where we find the seat of judgement for our work. Choices about what is right used to be made in fear and trembling of the judgement of God, beyond this life. Now we make those choices, also, for the judgements of the referee, interview panel, or the Independent Safeguarding Authority. Each choice affects our *curriculum vitae*.

Balancing codes and virtues

I have introduced you to two big themes of ethics: virtues of behaviour and codes of practice. Virtues are important because they appeal to our inner self. We judge ourselves and the virtues give us the themes we look at. They can give guides to our moral behaviour and we can make wider links to other people who might express one of the virtues so clearly that in that area they inspire us, or become our role model. The sometimes fragmented nature of our working lives means that the virtues can allow us to define the story of our own lives in relation to others. That personal insight can be empowering.

But codes are important too. The best rules are the ones that you can get to work. When they work they reinforce the authority of the body that sets and carries them out. Our codes are lists that recognise the power of conversation, democratic agreement, and our capacity for making hopeful groups and networks that will nurture and build just ideals for all of us – in the teeth of selfish behaviours. By building phrases that many use we make better noises to fill the air than the unsubtle and destructive noise of war, or the silence of ruins. Codes are iterative: if you don't like parts of them they are open to improvement by consultation, campaign and conversation.

Codes are needed in services for the vulnerable – and young people remain vulnerable in our societies. We used to rely on virtues, but they were essentially interior matters to be discussed with a counsellor, confessor, or non-managerial supervisor. But professionals who deal with people need to be more explicitly accountable than that. In the early 1990s I worked in a group to develop guidelines on child abuse for the Church of England's bishops. Only two of the 43 diocesan bishops we asked thought that the secrecy of the confession and forgiveness should take precedence, and they were persuaded to change their mind and agree to the code we had developed. On the other side of the Atlantic, in Boston, the cost of abuse continued to be counted in 2002 with the resignation of Cardinal Law and a huge payment in compensation to young people abused by priests committed to various virtues. Codes articulate explicitly so that professionals can be precisely accountable. It may be that the virtues will be helpful for each potential youth worker to judge their own interest and suitability for the driving moral purposes of youth work. It may be that we could only use the codes to explore the more external and developmental behaviour of youth workers who are learning to be professionals in university courses.

Linking ethical ideas

At its best, youth work has stakeholders who agree why the work needs doing and these stakeholders are broadly enough spread in a community to ensure support. Often youth work has been happy to behave like a grumpy adolescent: off on their own muttering that no one loves them, which becomes truer the more it goes on. Albemarle released financial capital to boost the youth service (1960, p111). We need, in the face of widespread social criticism of young people, to build social capital for youth work. This social capital needs to be bridging: between different social groups, rather than bonding (just among youth workers). I will show three ways in which bridges can be built.

A Parisian school

At the entrance in the Rue Vivienne, the school declares in large letters 'République Française' and the three values of the secular state expressed in Robespierre's motto for the state: Liberté, Égalité, Fraternité. Since 3 April 2004 there has been a memorial on the wall by the door for all to read as they go in:

> Remember the pupils of this school deported between 1942 and 1944 because they were born Jewish; innocent victims of the Nazi barbarism with the complicity of the Vichy government.

> They were exterminated in the death camps. 140 of the children had lived in the 2nd Arrondissement [District of Paris].

> Never forget them.

Public statements

Schools are local statements of the democratic will. The values of republican life express the core of the French state: Freedom, Equality, Brotherhood (even on girls' schools). The selection of those children contradicted all three values. The phrasing of the memorial (used across Paris), rebuilds those bonds of shared value.

- 'Deported' links these children to the French who were also deported to slave labour and who have been remembered, for example, in the 1962 memorial on the Ile de la Cité.

- 'Barbarism' links to Article 1 of the 1946 constitution which refers to *the victory of free people over the regimes that enslaved and degraded humanity*. (Pecheul, 2001, p48)

- The reference to the complicity of the Vichy regime has taken 60 years of difficult debates: *How can one explain the complicity of the Vichy regime in the Final Solution*?

(Rousso, 1992, p93)

Questions
- *What is the value of a public statement like this memorial?*

- *How does it affect an understanding of children's rights?*

- *What links can you make to your experience?*

Linking the NYA code and UN Convention on the Rights of the Child

The UN Convention contributes to young people's legislation and policy in the UK. Youth workers can build bridges between the ethical principles for our own work to the language and values expressed in Articles of the Convention. Because they are about the rights of young people they apply to all the first four principles in the code. Here is how we might link the articles to the code.

- NYA Code 1: Treat young people with respect.
  UN Code: Articles 1, 2, 3, 6, 7, 8, 16, 21, 23, 37, and 39.

- NYA Code 2: Respect young people's rights to make their own decisions and choices
  UN Code: Articles11, 12, 13, 14, 15, 17, 30, and 31.

- NYA Code 3: Promote and ensure the welfare and safety of young people.
  UN Code: Articles 9, 18, 19, 20, 24, 25, 27, 28, 29, 32, 33, 34, 35, 36, 38, 40.

- NYA Code 4: Contribute towards the promotion of social justice for young people.
  UN Code: Articles 4, 5, 10, 22, 26, 41.

- NYA Code 7: Develop and maintain the required skills and competence to do the job
  UN Code Article 3 refers to the training and qualification of the staff.

- NYA Code 8: Work for conditions in agencies where these principles are discussed, evaluated and upheld.
  UN Code Articles 43, 44 and 45 refer to the supporting work of implementing and monitoring the UN Code.

ACTIVITY 9.9

Questions

- *Discuss whether you agree with the suggested links.*

- *Develop arguments for better links.*

- *Do the Articles show any weaknesses in the NYA code?*

- *Suggest improvements that might be made to the NYA code.*

NYA Code and Nolan (1994)

The second part of the NYA Code focuses on professional behaviour, the role of the worker specifically. Youth work is set in the public domain and it makes sense to link the work we do with the recent debates about 'Standards in Public Life'. The Nolan Commission reported (1994)

- *These principles (see The Seven Principles of Public Life) apply to all aspects of public life. The Committee has set them out here for the benefit of all who serve the public in any way.*

- *More needs to be done to promote and reinforce standards of conduct in public bodies, in particular through guidance and training, including induction training.*

The NYA code 5 and 6 cover the same areas of boundaries and accountability addressed by the Nolan principles.

ACTIVITY **9.10**

The seven principles of public life

These principles apply to all public servants: MPs, Council Officers, NHS staff etc.

1 *Selflessness: take decisions solely in terms of the public interest. Do not do so in order to gain financial or other material benefits for yourself, family, or friends.*

2 *Integrity: do not place yourself under any financial or other obligation to outside individuals or organisations that might influence you in the performance of your official duties.*

3 *Objectivity: in carrying out public business, including making public appointments, awarding contracts, or recommending individuals for rewards and benefits, you should make choices on merit.*

4 *Accountability: you are accountable for your decisions and actions to the public and must submit yourself to whatever scrutiny is appropriate.*

5 *Openness: you should be as open as possible about all the decisions and actions that you take. You should give reasons for decisions and restrict information only when the wider public interest clearly demands.*

6 *Honesty: you have a duty to declare any private interests relating to your public duties and to take steps to resolve any conflicts arising in a way that protects the public interest.*

7 *Leadership: you should promote and support these principles by leadership and example.*

Questions

• *What would you do if a friend or relative applied for a job and you were on the short-listing, or interview group?*

• *Who are you accountable to, and how do you express this?*

• *How can you express leadership in promoting and supporting these principles?*

• *Have you used these principles before?*

Reviewing bridge building

Shared values can be encouraged by using the same words, same codes, and by being consistent. Youth workers can be the only public servants that people meet in their neighbourhood. We have the opportunity to promote and implement the rights of young people and the values we work to express. Perhaps we should also use the same set of values, for instance, in the National Occupational Standards to encourage consistency.

C H A P T E R   R E V I E W

My ambition in writing this book was that you might find it useful in your youth work. Perhaps that you would come back to it as you do your work and see how what you are trying to do can be understood, and how you can think things through. Ethics is for the long term, what you do in your youth work career. Passing a module, writing a reflective comment, joining in with a seminar discussion are important first steps, but they are more artificial than what you will have to do. Getting a responsible job, writing funding bids, replying to a public meeting are what youth workers end up doing and ethics needs to be robust in these settings.

There are themes that you will have picked up that seem to me to underpin ethical youth work.

- The priority of the young person.

- Importance of the parents/key carers.

- Work with partners who are able to contribute professional benefit to the young people.

- Setting the work in a wider context – remember history and think about the whole world.

- Youth work is an educational activity: plan learning for life for young people.

- Advocate what is right.

It is a lot to hold together and you can't just wing it. Try to keep preparing on paper and recording afterwards what happened. Accountability in public means that people come back to you long after the event and want to know what happened. A short note at the end of the day can save a lot of trouble later on.

Youth work allows adults to take on some old tasks in society. There have always been bridges built for children into adult life. For centuries these were called apprenticeships, pupillages, novitiates, and so on. Young people are vulnerable to being excluded from adult life, and it seems to suit the generation for whom Albemarle reported to hang onto their jobs by excluding the potential of young people by criticising their exam results, doubting their social skills, and restricting aspects of their lives. Adults doing youth work can help build bridges to help transitions to adult life.

FURTHER READING

Banks, S (ed) (1999) *Ethical issues in youth work.* London: Routledge. This well established book is particularly valuable for the seven worked examples.

Faulks, S (1999) *Charlotte Gray.* London: Vintage. A page turning novel (and film) of life in Nazi occupied France that includes vivid descriptions of the deportation of children via Drancy.

REFERENCES

Albemarle Report (1960) *The youth service in England and Wales.* London: HMSO.

Aquinas, T (1920) *Summa theologica* (the first part of the second section). Dominican Order.

Aristotle (2000) *Nicomachean ethics,* edited by Crisp, R. Cambridge: Cambridge University Press.

Bonhoeffer, D (1995) *Ethics*. New York: Touchstone.

CBF (1996) *Tomorrow is another country.* London: Board of Education.

Davie, G (2002) *Europe: the exceptional case.* London: DLT.

Davies, N (1996) *Europe*. Oxford: Oxford University Press.

Hume, D (1739–40) *A treatise of human nature: being an attempt to introduce the experimental method of reasoning into moral subjects*. London: John Noon.

Kant, I (1997) *Groundwork of the metaphysics of morals*. Cambridge: Cambridge University Press.

MacIntyre, A (1985) *After virtue*. London: Duckworth.

Middleton, J, in Petit-Zeman, S (2006) *How to be an even better chair*. Harlow: Pearson.

Nietzsche, F (2002) *Beyond good and evil*. Cambridge: Cambridge University Press.

Nolan (1994) First report of the committee on standards in public life. London: TSO.

Obama, B (2007) *Dreams from my father*. Edinburgh: Canongate.

Pecheul, A (2001) Les dates clefs de la protection des droits de l'homme en France. Paris: Ellipses.

Rawls, J (1971) *A theory of justice*. Cambridge Massachusetts: Belknap Press of Harvard University.

Rousso, H (1992) *Les années noires*. Paris: Gallimard.

Smith, JE (1967) Rights, in Macquarrie, J.A (ed) *Dictionary of Christian Ethics*. London: SCM Press.

UNICEF (2006) *The state of the world's children 2007* UNICEF: New York.

Index